KS3 ENGLISH ANTHOLOGY

DETECTIVES

Paula Adair

Series editor: Jane Sheldon

HODDER
EDUCATION
AN HACHETTE UK COMPANY

Although every effort has been made to ensure that website addresses are correct at time of going to press, Hodder Education cannot be held responsible for the content of any website mentioned in this book. It is sometimes possible to find a relocated web page by typing in the address of the home page for a website in the URL window of your browser.

Hachette UK's policy is to use papers that are natural, renewable and recyclable products and made from wood grown in well-managed forests and other controlled sources. The logging and manufacturing processes are expected to conform to the environmental regulations of the country of origin.

Orders: please contact Hachette UK Distribution, Hely Hutchinson Centre, Milton Road, Didcot, Oxfordshire, OX11 7HH. Telephone: +44 (0)1235 827827. Email education@hachette.co.uk Lines are open from 9 a.m. to 5 p.m., Monday to Friday. You can also order through our website: www.hoddereducation.co.uk

ISBN: 978 1 5104 7731 5

© Paula Adair 2020

First published in 2020 by
Hodder Education,
An Hachette UK Company
Carmelite House
50 Victoria Embankment
London EC4Y 0DZ

www.hoddereducation.co.uk

Impression number   10 9 8 7 6 5 4 3 2

Year   2024 2023 2022

Cover artwork by Dylan Gibson http://www.dylangibsonillustration.co.uk/

Typeset by Integra Software Services Pvt. Ltd., Pondicherry, India.

Printed and bound by CPI Group (UK) Ltd, Croydon, CR0 4YY

A catalogue record for this title is available from the British Library.

MIX
Paper | Supporting
responsible forestry
FSC™ C104740

Contents

Introduction   3

Fiction   6

1 Bug Muldoon and the Garden of Fear   6
2 An Inspector Calls   10
3 A Study in Scarlet   14
4 Lamb to the Slaughter   18
5 The Adventure of the Final Problem   22
6 The No. 1 Ladies' Detective Agency   26
7 The Mysterious Affair at Styles   30
8 The Murders in the Rue Morgue   34

Non-fiction   38

9 In Search of Sherlock   38
10 'Poirot has been my best friend'   42
11 Jonathan Creek   46
12 'I'm a homicide detective in the LAPD'   50
13 Sherlock Gnomes   54
14 Real Life Detectives   58
15 The Timeless Secret of Nancy Drew   62
16 Police Now   66

Poetry   70

17 The Bloodhound   70
18 What Has Happened to Lulu?   74
19 Macavity the Mystery Cat   78
20 Inspector Tweede   82
21 Flannan Isle   86
22 About His Person   90
23 The Man Who Finds Out His Son Has Become a Thief   94
24 A Case of Murder   98

Key terms   102

Acknowledgements

pp. 6–7 from *Bug Muldoon: The Garden of Fear* by Paul Shipton, ISBN 9780198328469, © 2008, Oxford University Press. Used with permission via PLS Clear; **pp. 18–19** from 'Lamb to the Slaughter (A Roald Dahl Short Story)' by Roald Dahl, ISBN 9781405911030, © The Roald Dahl Story Company Limited, 1953. Jonathan Cape Ltd & Penguin Books Ltd. Used with permission from David Higham Associates; **pp. 26–27** United States, its Territories and Possessions, Republic of the Philippines, Canada, Open Market: Excerpt(s) from THE NO. 1 LADIES' DETECTIVE AGENCY by Alexander McCall Smith, copyright © 1998, 2005 by Alexander McCall Smith. Used by permission of Anchor Books, an imprint of the Knopf Doubleday Publishing Group, a division of Penguin Random House LLC. All rights reserved; UK and Commonwealth (excl. Canada) and European Union: From 'THE NO. 1 LADIES' DETECTIVE AGENCY' by Alexander McCall Smith, copyright © 1998, 2005 by Alexander McCall Smith. Used with permission from David Higham Associates; **pp. 38–39** from 'Elementary, My Dear' by Shreya Sen Handley, previously published by National Geographic under the title 'In Search of Sherlock', October 2014; **pp. 42–43** from David Suchet interview: 'Poirot has been my best friend' *The Telegraph*, 30 October 2013, © Telegraph Media Group Limited, https://www.telegraph.co.uk/culture/tvandradio/10374111/David-Suchet-interview-Poirot-has-been-my-best-friend.html. Reproduced with permission; **pp. 46–47** from 'Jonathan Creek: Natalie Haynes's guide to TV detectives #21 by Natalie Haynes'. Published on 27 November 2012. https://www.theguardian.com/tv-and-radio/tvandradioblog/2012/nov/27/jonathan-creek-natalie-haynes-tv-detectives. Reproduced with permission from Guardian News & Media Limited; **pp. 50–51** from 'I'm a homicide detective in the LAPD. What do you want to know? Christopher Barling' by Ruth Spencer. Published on 25 July 2013. https://www.theguardian.com/commentisfree/2013/jul/25/homicide-detective-lapd-daily-life. Reproduced with permission from Guardian News & Media Limited; **pp. 54–55** from 'Sherlock Gnomes Review' by Nick Allen, published on 23 March 2018. https://www.rogerebert.com/reviews/sherlock-gnomes-2018. Reproduced with permission from Ebert Digital LLC; **pp. 58–59 Sophie Hannah**, from 'Real Life Private Detectives', https://sophiehannah.com/real-life-private-detectives/. © 2018, Sophie Hannah. Reproduced by permission of the author c/o Rogers, Coleridge & White Ltd., 20 Powis Mews, London W11 1JN; **pp. 66–67** National Detective Programme, © Police Now; **pp. 74–75** from 'What Has Happened to Lulu?' by Charles Causley, © David Higham Associates Limited, On Behalf of Georgia Glover; **pp. 78–77** from 'Macavity the Mystery Cat' by T S Eliot, © FABER & FABER, The Estate of T S Eliot. Used with permission from Faber & Faber Ltd; **pp. 82–83** 'Inspector Tweede' by Robert L Hinshaw, 2011, © Robert L Hinshaw. Reproduced with kind permission of the author; **pp. 86–87** from 'Flannan Isle' by Wilfrid Wilson Gibson, © Judy Greenway, reproduced with permission from the Trustees of the Wilfred Gibson Estate; **p. 90** 'About His Person' by Simon Armitage, © Simon Armitage. Reproduced with permission from Faber & Faber Ltd; **p. 94** 'The Man Who Finds Out His Son Has Become a Thief' by Raymond Souster is reprinted from *Collected Poems of Raymond Souster* by permission of Oberon Press; **pp. 98–99** from *Collected Poems 1950–1993*, 'A Case of Murder' by Vernon Scannell, © The estate of Vernon Scannell (Faber). Used with permission.

Photo credits

p. 1 *t* Public domain/https://commons.wikimedia.org/wiki/File:Sherlock_Holmes_and_Professor_Moriarty_at_the_Reichenbach_Falls.jpg, *m* © ITV/Shutterstock, *b* © Omega - stock.adobe.com; **p. 3** © PictureLux / The Hollywood Archive / Alamy Stock Photo; **p. 4** *ml* © Everett Collection Inc / Alamy Stock Photo, *mm* © PictureLux / The Hollywood Archive / Alamy Stock Photo, *mr* © Pictorial Press Ltd / Alamy Stock Photo, *b* © Everett Collection Inc / Alamy Stock Photo; **p. 5** *t* © Getty Images/iStockphoto/Thinkstock, *m* © The History Collection / Alamy Stock Photo; **p. 6** ©yod77 – stock.adobe.com; **p. 8** ©Klaus Eppele – stock.adobe.com; **p. 10** © Bettina Strenske / Alamy Stock Photo; **p. 14** © snaptitude - stock.adobe.com; **p. 18** ©Vladimir – stock.adobe.com; **p. 22** Public domain/https://commons.wikimedia.org/wiki/File:Sherlock_Holmes_and_Professor_Moriarty_at_the_Reichenbach_Falls.jpg; **pp. 26** © Little, Brown Book Group; **p. 27** ©my_stock – stock.adobe.com; **p. 29** ©Christian - stock.adobe.com **p. 30** © Everett Collection Inc / Alamy Stock Photo; **p. 34** Library of Congress Prints and Photographs Division Washington, D.C./LC-USZ62-10610; **p. 37** © Marco Saracco – stock.adobe.com; **pp. 38 and 41** © John Warburton-Lee Photography / Alamy Stock Photo; **p. 42** © ITV/Shutterstock; **p. 46** © Trinity Mirror / Mirrorpix / Alamy Stock Photo; **pp. 50 and 53** © Shutterstock / Elliott Cowand Jr; **p. 54** © Paramount Pictures / Everett Collection Inc / Alamy Stock Photo; **p. 58** © Getty Images/iStockphoto/Thinkstock; **p. 62** © PictureLux / The Hollywood Archive / Alamy Stock Photo; **p. 66** *t* © Mikhail Palinchak/123RF.com, *m* Courtesy of Police Now; **p. 70** © Alexey Kuznetsov - stock.adobe.com; **p. 73** © frank1crayon - stock.adobe.com; **p. 74** © canbedone - stock.adobe.com; **p. 75** © Alexandr Vlassyuk - stock.adobe.com; **p. 77** © Alexandr Vasilyev - stock.adobe.com; **p. 78** © Omega - stock.adobe.com; **p. 82** © PrettyVectors - stock.adobe.com; **p. 89** © peshkov - stock.adobe.com; **p. 90** *t* ©iweta0077 - stock.adobe.com, *b* © DenisProduction.com - stock.adobe.com; **p. 93** © DenisProduction.com - stock.adobe.com; **p. 94** © Mihail - stock.adobe.com; **p. 98** © Eric Isselée - stock.adobe.com.

Introduction

What do you think of when you hear the word 'detective'? You may have read a book about a detective solving crimes, watched a film where a detective outwits a villain or perhaps you are the family champion at Cluedo! Maybe you have thought that you would like to become a detective yourself one day and become famous by solving the 'crime of the century'! There are several reasons why you may enjoy detective stories or films. Perhaps you enjoy the hunt for evidence and solving clues and puzzles, or maybe you enjoy the thrill of mystery and danger.

However, have you actually thought about what a detective is and what detectives actually do?

The dictionary definition of a 'detective' is 'a person, often a police officer, whose occupation is to investigate and solve crimes'.

There are different types of detectives, such as:

- police detectives
- private investigators
- amateur sleuths.

In this book, you will be reading about fictional and real-life detectives and exploring what makes a successful detective story. You might be surprised by how many fictional detectives you have heard of!

Kid detectives: The Famous Five

You might have read about The Famous Five. These fictional detectives are four children (Julian, Dick, Anne and Georgina) and their dog (Timmy), who always get caught up in adventures or find a mystery to solve – whether on a treasure island, in a caravan, at sea or on Demon's Rock. Beginning in 1942, the British author Enid Blyton wrote 22 books about The Famous Five.

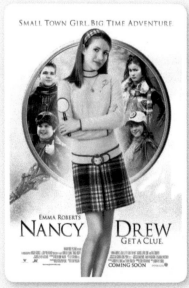

NOW TRY THIS

Undertake some research to find out the titles of the 22 books. Which of the titles do you think sounds the most exciting or the scariest? Be prepared to explain your choice to your class.

Nancy Drew and the Hardy Boys

The Nancy Drew Mysteries were a series of books by an American writer about a clever, confident and independent teenager who had a knack for solving crimes and mysteries. Linked to these stories are the Hardy Boys – two fictional brothers who solved the cases that adults couldn't.

▲ Nancy Drew as she appears in a 2007 film

Sherlock Holmes

Probably the most famous fictional detective of all time is Sherlock Holmes – in fact some people even thought he was real. However, Sherlock Holmes was a character created by the Scottish writer Sir Arthur Conan Doyle in the late nineteenth and early twentieth centuries. The character lived at 221B Baker Street in London and his stories are narrated by his trusted friend Watson. There are many famous stories about Sherlock Holmes and his crime fighting skills.

NOW TRY THIS

How many of the Sherlock Holmes stories can you name? Who is Holmes's arch enemy?

If you are not sure, you could undertake some research about the character.

Here are some images of actors who have played the role of Sherlock Holmes. Which is the closest to how you imagine him to look? Share your opinion with your partner.

Using the pictures to help you and drawing on your own knowledge, list some of the clothes and props that are associated with Sherlock Holmes. What do these suggest to us about the type of character he is? Share your opinions with your partner.

Auguste Dupin

Interestingly, Sir Arthur Conan Doyle based his character of Sherlock Holmes on another fictional detective, Auguste Dupin, created by the American writer Edgar Allan Poe. Dupin appears in several stories and perhaps the most famous one is *Murders in the Rue Morgue*. Arthur Conan Doyle said that Poe 'was the model for all time'. What you think he might have meant by this?

Hercule Poirot

▲ Hercule Poirot

Another famous fictional detective is Hercule Poirot, created by the British writer Agatha Christie. He is probably best known for his immense moustache and his intelligence in solving tricky cases.

NOW TRY THIS

Make a list of adjectives you would use to describe a detective, for example intelligent, determined.

Real life detectives

Almost every time you read a newspaper or watch the news on television, you will hear stories of real-life detectives and police officers solving crimes, saving lives and helping people. However, the day-to-day life of a real detective is probably not as exciting or glamorous as the fictional detectives you read about.

▲ A detective conducting an interview

NOW TRY THIS

With a partner, research some of the real-life detectives from the list below. Produce a fact file for the detective(s) you find the most interesting.

- ✪ Allan Pinkerton
- ✪ Ignatius Pollaky
- ✪ William J Burns
- ✪ Frank Hamer and Maney Gault.

Wyatt Earp (1848–1929)

Of course, officers of the law have been keeping citizens safe and protecting the innocent for centuries. Many of these officers were known as 'sheriffs' in the American Old West. One of these real-life heroes was Wyatt Earp, who was most famous for the gunfight at the OK Corral.

NOW TRY THIS

Research facts about the OK Corral gunfight and write a front-page newspaper story describing the dramatic events of the shoot-out.

Imagine you interview Wyatt Earp after the shoot-out. With a partner, write a script of the interview.

▲ Wyatt Earp

Detectives in poetry

Poets across the ages have written about the work detectives do and their skill in solving mysteries. Probably some of the earliest detective poems are in the form of ballads (a narrative poem in verses). Some of these poems are *Lord Randall* and *The Ballad of Charlotte Dymond*.

In these ballads, the murderer is often not revealed and the reader is meant to act as the detective to try to come up with an answer.

In this book, you will come across some ballads, so to help you become used to this genre, carry out some research into where ballads originated.

Look for some ballads and work out what they have in common. You can even try to create your own mystery ballad with a partner!

WIDER READING SUGGESTIONS

If you want to read some detective fiction, you could try:

- ✪ *Agatha Oddly: The Silver Serpent*, Lena Jones
- ✪ The *Murder Most Unladylike* series, Robin Stevens
- ✪ *The ABC Murders*, Agatha Christie
- ✪ *The Sign of Four*, Sir Arthur Conan Doyle.

Section 1: Fiction

1 Bug Muldoon and the Garden of Fear
By Paul Shipton

▲ 'Bug. The name is Bug.'

LEARNING OBJECTIVES

- ⊗ To recognise implicit ideas in a text.
- ⊗ To explore the writer's techniques.
- ⊗ To comment on the writer's presentation of characters.

CONTEXT

Bug Muldoon is a fictional detective created by Paul Shipton but he is a very unusual one. In fact, he is actually a beetle and his cases are set in the world of the garden, with insects as his clients. Shipton deliberately makes Bug sound and act like an American detective from novels and television shows that were popular in the 1950s, especially the detective Phillip Marlowe, who was created by the novelist Raymond Chandler.

The following extract is from Chapter 1, where Bug Muldoon is approached by three worried earwigs to help find their missing brother.

The earwigs have gone to Bug Muldoon's office to ask for help in finding their missing brother.

'Mr Muldoon?' he asked.

'Bug. The name is Bug.' (It makes me tense when people call me Mister.) 'What do you guys want?'

The big one introduced himself as Larry. Nice name, I thought. Larry did all the talking. The other two nodded their heads in encouragement.

'It's our brother, Eddie,' said Larry. 'He's gone missing …' The other two jiggled their heads.

They needn't have bothered – this sounded like a story I'd heard a million times before. A bug going missing isn't exactly big news in the Garden. Still, the three earwigs looked like they expected me to ask some questions, so I did. Anything to oblige a client.

'When did he disappear?' I asked. It seemed like as good a place to start as any.

The words and sentences used by Bug make him sound like an American detective.

The writer uses an ellipsis to show that the earwigs are nervous and anxious about what has happened to their brother.

Bug doesn't sound particularly interested in the case so far.

6

Larry's antennae waved nervously as he spoke. He was an edgy kinda guy.

'Late last night was the last time we saw him …'

'And did he say anything – any indication that he was going somewhere?'

Larry hesitated. It gave one of the other two a chance to chip in.

'He said he was going to the meadow,' he blurted.

Larry shook his head. 'Eddie was all talk, he'd never really do it –'

I nodded, but I knew better. How many innocent young insects had I met who dreamed of a better life outside of this Garden – in the meadow on the other side of the stream? They thought that life would be easier. They thought they could spend their days there without always worrying about being eaten by a spider, a bird or just by the bug next door. Now, I like fairy stories as much as the next beetle, but I knew one thing: life was as hard in the meadow as it was in this hell-hole of a Garden that we call home. If Eddie had struck out for the meadow there was no guarantee he had made it. Still, I didn't see any point in turning away clients.

'Could be he headed for the meadow, could be he got stuck along the way. If the second is true, I might be able to find him,' I said.

I told them I would look for Eddie, or at least try to dig up any information on where he had gone. I told them my daily fee – plus expenses – and they didn't look too worried.

Bug sounds very experienced and seems to think this case will not be unusual.

Bug decides to take the case as he has to make a living.

It sounds as if Bug thinks he knows what has happened. Do you think this will be a straightforward case? Remember that this conversation is from Chapter 1.

Bug is a realistic character and knows that life is hard for the insects, no matter where they live.

GLOSSARY

Tense: uncomfortable or stressed
Jiggled: wiggled
Oblige: please
Edgy: nervous
Struck out for: made a break for
Fee: charge
Expenses: costs

SKILLS FOCUS

✔ Understand how writers create effect through language and technique.
✔ Consider how the choice of language affects our opinion.
✔ Consider how the writer uses dialogue to create tension in the extract.

LOOK CLOSER

1 Read the extract again. What do we learn about the three earwigs and their relationships with each other? Think about:
- ○ how they behave
- ○ what they say
- ○ the language that the writer uses to describe them.

2 What impression does the writer create of Bug Muldoon here? You can use a copy of this table to help you.

Quotation	Effect: This suggests that ...
'Bug. The name is Bug.'	
'What do you guys want?'	
'this sounded like a story I'd heard a million times before.'	
'Anything to oblige a client.'	
'I nodded, but I knew better.'	

Now write a paragraph to answer the question, using the information from your table to help you.

3 '"He said he was going to the meadow," he blurted.' What does the verb 'blurted' suggest?

4 The writer creates tension in the passage by using more dialogue than description. Pick out two pieces of dialogue and think about how they create tension. Think about:
- ○ the length of the sentences
- ○ the punctuation used.

◀ 'Larry's antennae waved nervously as he spoke'

NOW TRY THIS

1 Bug Muldoon is a good detective. What characteristics (typical features) does he show here that prove that he is good at his job? Write a list of these characteristics and add any ideas of your own from other things that you have seen or read about detectives.

2 Imagine you are replying to a job advertisement to become a detective with the 'Ace Detective Agency'. Write your letter of application for this job. Think about:
- a formal letter layout
- how you found out about the job
- why you would be suitable for this job
- why you would like this job.

3 With a partner, share your lists about the typical characteristics of a good detective from Now Try This Question 1. Discuss what you consider to be the most important qualities for a detective and rank them in order from 1 to 5. Be prepared to explain and defend your ideas to the class. Remember to use full sentences when speaking and use connectives like 'because', 'since' and 'therefore' to support your ideas.

FAST FINISHERS

With your partner and using all the information you have gathered from this chapter, write a script where you are interviewing your partner for a job as a detective. Decide who will be the interviewer and who will be the interviewee. Write down the questions you will ask and your partner can prepare his/her answers. You might want to use these lines as a starting point:

INTERVIEWER: Good morning, Miss Smith. Please sit down.

APPLICANT: Thank you.

INTERVIEWER: I see that you have applied for the position of ...

Practise acting out the interview.

❓ PRACTICE QUESTION

Read the extract again. Choose **four** statements below which are **true**. [4 marks]

- Copy out the ones that you think are true.
- Choose a maximum of four true statements.

A Bug is asked to investigate the case of a missing ant. ☐

B Bug's surname is Muldoon. ☐

C The missing brother is called Larry. ☐

D The missing brother was last seen at lunchtime on the previous day. ☐

E Eddie said his brother had been going to the meadow. ☐

F Larry does most of the talking for the earwigs. ☐

G The earwigs live in the city. ☐

H Bug is used to dealing with cases like this. ☐

2 An Inspector Calls

By J B Priestley

▲ The mysterious Inspector Goole

LEARNING OBJECTIVES

⚙ To recognise implicit ideas in a text.

⚙ To comment on the writer's presentation of characters.

⚙ To understand the social and historical context.

CONTEXT

An Inspector Calls is a play written by J B Priestley (1894–1984) and it is set in Edwardian England in 1912. It tells the story of the wealthy Birling family who are somehow involved in the death of a young girl called Eva Smith. A mysterious police inspector arrives at the Birlings' home to question them about their involvement with the dead girl.

The following extract is from Act 1 of the play and is at the point where Inspector Goole arrives to question members of the Birling family.

The inspector need not be a big man but he creates at once an impression of massiveness, solidity and purposefulness. He is a man in his fifties, dressed in a plain darkish suit of the period. He speaks carefully, weightily, and has a disconcerting habit of looking hard at the person he addresses before actually speaking.

INSPECTOR Mr Birling?

BIRLING Yes. Sit down, Inspector.

INSPECTOR [*Sitting*] Thank you, sir.

BIRLING Have a glass of port – or a little whisky?

INSPECTOR No, thank you, Mr Birling. I'm on duty.

BIRLING You're new, aren't you?

INSPECTOR Yes sir. Only recently transferred.

BIRLING I thought you must be. I was an alderman for years – and Lord Mayor two years ago – and I'm still on the Bench – so I know the Brumley police officers pretty well – and I thought I'd never seen you before.

> The stage directions tell the audience how the Inspector enters the Birlings' home. He is described as being a very serious man.

> Mr Birling is polite to the Inspector and offers him some refreshments.

> The Inspector reveals very little information about himself.

10

INSPECTOR Quite so.

BIRLING Well what can I do for you? Some trouble about a warrant?

> Mr Birling is confused about why the Inspector has come there.

INSPECTOR No, Mr Birling.

BIRLING [*After a pause, with a touch of impatience*] Well, what is it then?

INSPECTOR I'd like some information, if you don't mind, Mr Birling. Two hours ago a young woman died in the Infirmary …

> The Inspector reveals that a young woman has died in hospital.

BIRLING [*Rather impatiently*] Yes, yes, horrible business. But I don't understand why you should come here Inspector –

> What does this dash suggest about Birling's attitude to the Inspector here?

INSPECTOR [*Cutting through massively*] I've been round to the room she had, and she'd left a sort of diary there. Like a lot of these young women who get into various kinds of trouble, she'd used more than one name. But her original name – her real name – was Eva Smith.

BIRLING [*Thoughtfully*] Eva Smith?

INSPECTOR Do you remember her, Mr Birling?

BIRLING [*Slowly*] No – I seem to remember hearing that name – Eva Smith – somewhere. But it doesn't convey anything to me. And I don't see where I come into this.

> The dashes (–) show that Birling's speech has slowed down as he struggles to remember the girl.

INSPECTOR She was employed in your works at the time.

BIRLING Oh – that's it, is it? Well, we've several hundred young women there y'know, and they keep changing.

> In England in the 1900s, many women worked in factories for very little money and would often move to another factory in the hope of earning more. The factory owners, like Birling, were unconcerned about the welfare of their workers and took very little interest in them.

INSPECTOR This young woman, Eva Smith, was a bit out of the ordinary. I found a photograph of her in her lodgings. Perhaps you'd remember her from that.

The inspector takes a photograph, about postcard size, out of his pocket and goes to Birling. Both Gerald and Eric rise to have a look at the photograph, but the inspector interposes himself between them and the photograph. They are surprised and rather annoyed. Birling stares hard and with recognition at the photograph, which the inspector then replaces in his pocket.

GERALD [*Showing annoyance*] Any particular reason why I shouldn't see this girl's photograph, Inspector?

INSPECTOR [*Coolly, looking hard at him*] There might be.

> A tense atmosphere is created here as the Inspector doesn't reveal any more information and keeps the characters in suspense.

GLOSSARY

Purposefulness: confidence

Disconcerting: making someone feel uncomfortable or uneasy

Addresses: speaks to

Alderman: member of the council

On the Bench: a magistrate

Warrant: official police document

Infirmary: hospital

Convey: mean

Lodgings: the place where she lived

Gerald and Eric: Gerald is Birling's future son-in-law; Eric is Birling's son

Interposes: stands between

Coolly: calmly

SKILLS FOCUS

✔ Understand how writers create effect through language and technique.
✔ Consider how the writer creates character.
✔ Consider how the writer creates suspense in the extract.

LOOK CLOSER

1. Read the stage directions at the start of the extract again. What impression do you have of the Inspector here? Think about:
   - his appearance and the clothes he wears
   - his behaviour
   - the language that the writer uses to describe him.

2. What important positions has Mr Birling held in the town?

3. How does the writer show that Mr Birling gradually becomes more annoyed with the Inspector? Fill in a copy of this table to help you track through Mr Birling's feelings.

Quotation	Effect: This suggests that ...
'Sit down, Inspector.'	
'Have a glass of port – or a little whisky?'	
'You're new, aren't you?'	
'Well, what can I do for you?'	
'With a touch of impatience'	

4. Now, using your table as a plan, write two paragraphs answering the following question: How does Mr Birling behave towards the Inspector and how do his feelings change as the extract develops?

NOW TRY THIS

1 At the start of the extract, the Inspector is described as being an intimidating character. Write a short description of a character who is a bit scary or menacing. Think about:

- ✪ what your character looks like
- ✪ what your character wears
- ✪ how your character speaks and moves.

Remember to use interesting adjectives and adverbs where you can.

2 Write a diary entry from the Inspector's point of view, describing his meeting with Mr Birling. Remember to write in first person narrative.

You might want to use this line as a starting point for the Inspector's diary:

> What an unpleasant and uncooperative man Mr Birling is!

FAST FINISHERS

Now write a diary entry from the point of view of Mr Birling. You might wish to start:

> I have never been treated so badly in my own home! Who does that Inspector think he is? I've a good mind to report him ...

3 With a partner, imagine what will happen next in the interview between Mr Birling and the Inspector. Think about what you have found out about the two characters so far and try to create tension between them. Remember to:

- ✪ set your interview out in script form
- ✪ include stage directions to describe the actions of the characters and to show the tone of their voices and their moods.

Be prepared to act out the meeting in front of your class.

❓ PRACTICE QUESTION

Read the extract again. Choose **four** statements below which are **true**. [4 marks]

- ✪ Copy out the ones that you think are true.
- ✪ Choose a maximum of four true statements.

A The Inspector is a shy and timid character. ☐

B The Inspector wears dark coloured clothes. ☐

C Mr Birling is a police officer. ☐

D The Inspector has a glass of whisky. ☐

E Mr Birling has been a Lord Mayor. ☐

F The local police officers are well known to Mr Birling. ☐

G A young woman died six hours ago. ☐

H The Inspector uses short, blunt sentences. ☐

3 A Study in Scarlet

By Arthur Conan Doyle

▲ Sherlock Holmes with his trademark accessories: a pipe and magnifying glass

LEARNING OBJECTIVES

- ⊗ To recognise implicit and explicit ideas in a text.
- ⊗ To explore the writer's techniques.
- ⊗ To comment on the writer's presentation of characters.

CONTEXT

Sherlock Holmes is a famous fictional detective created by Sir Arthur Conan Doyle (1859–1930) during the Victorian period. Holmes lives in the fictitious 221B Baker Street in London and is helped by his trusted friend Dr Watson to solve mysterious and puzzling crimes. The most famous novels about Sherlock Holmes are *A Study in Scarlet*, *The Sign of Four* and *The Hound of the Baskervilles*. Like all successful crime fighters, Holmes has a deadly enemy, Professor Moriarty, and, in his final novel, Conan Doyle kills Sherlock off in a clifftop fight with Moriarty.

The following extract is from *A Study in Scarlet,* in which Sherlock Holmes reveals the identity of a murderer. It is told from the point of view of Dr Watson.

'Gentlemen,' he cried, with flashing eyes, 'let me introduce you to Mr. Jefferson Hope, the murderer of Enoch Drebber and of Joseph Stangerson.'

The whole thing occurred in a moment – so quickly that I had no time to realise it. I have a vivid recollection of that instant, of Holmes's triumphant expression and the ring of his voice, of the cabman's dazed, savage face, as he glared at the glittering handcuffs, which had appeared as if by magic upon his wrists. For a second or two we might have been a group of statues. Then with an inarticulate roar of fury, the prisoner wrenched himself free from Holmes's grasp, and hurled himself through the window. Woodwork and glass gave way before him; but before he got quite through, Gregson, Lestrade and Holmes sprang upon him like so many staghounds. He was dragged back into the room, and then commenced a terrific conflict. So powerful and so fierce was he that the four of us were shaken off

Sherlock Holmes announces the identity of the murderer as Jefferson Hope.

Everything happens very quickly and the writer shows a clear difference between the feelings of Sherlock Holmes and the murderer.

The writer uses violent verbs to show how the murderer becomes furious and tries to escape.

The writer uses the metaphor 'we might have been a group of statues'. What impression do you have of the characters and their behaviour here?

again and again. He appeared to have the convulsive strength of a man in an epileptic fit. His face and hands were terribly mangled by his passage through the glass, but loss of blood had no effect in diminishing his resistance. It was not until Lestrade succeeded in getting his hand inside his neckcloth and half-strangling him that we made him realise that his struggles were of no avail; and even then we felt no security until we had pinioned his feet as well as his hands. That done, we rose to our feet breathless and panting.

The murderer is very strong and resists arrest violently.

Eventually Sherlock Holmes and the policemen manage to overpower the murderer.

GLOSSARY

Triumphant: feeling pleased after winning something

Cabman: driver

Inarticulate: being unable to express ideas or feelings clearly

Staghounds: large dogs used for hunting deer

Convulsive: jerky, violent and uncontrollable movements

Epileptic: uncontrollable movements as if in a seizure

Diminishing: lessening

Lestrade: the name of a police inspector helping Sherlock Holmes

No avail: no use

Pinioned: restrained or tied up

SKILLS FOCUS

✔ Understand how writers create effect through language and technique.

✔ Consider how the choice of language affects our opinion.

✔ Consider how the writer creates excitement and tension in the extract.

LOOK CLOSER

1. Read the opening of the extract. The writer shows a clear difference between the detective and the murderer.
    - Holmes is described as having a 'triumphant expression'.
    - The murderer is described as having a 'dazed, savage face'.
    What impressions do you have of these characters?

2. The metaphor 'we might have been a group of statues' is used to describe the behaviour of the characters. Explain how they are behaving at this moment and why they are behaving in this way.

3. A few lines further on in the passage, the detectives jump on the criminal. The writer says that they 'sprang upon him like so many staghounds'. What impressions do you have of the characters' behaviour now?

4. Think about how the writer makes the passage tense and exciting.
    (a) Track through the passage from beginning to end and write down what actually happens and in what order the events take place. You can do this in point form.
    (b) Copy and complete the table on the next page to help organise your ideas.

Evidence from the text	Effect on the reader
'So quickly that I had no time to realise it'	
'the cabman's dazed, savage face'	
'for a second or two we might have been a group of statues'	
'the prisoner wrenched himself free'	
'hurled himself through the window'	
'then commenced a terrific conflict'	
'the four of us were shaken off again and again'	
'we rose to our feet breathless and panting'	

NOW TRY THIS

1 Imagine you are a newspaper reporter who has been asked to write a front-page newspaper exclusive about the arrest and capture of the dangerous criminal, Jefferson Hope. Remember to:
   - use a newspaper layout and a dramatic headline
   - find a suitable picture and caption to match the story
   - include an interview with Sherlock Holmes about the arrest
   - include the important information for the 5Ws – who, where, what, when, why
   - use details from this passage and make up any other details.

2 There are many synonyms for the word 'detective'. Look at the table below and decide whether these words are synonyms for the term 'detective' and how the dictionary explains them.

Word	Synonym: Yes or No	Dictionary definition
Mole		
Lawman		
Investigator		
Sleuth		

Villain		
Spy		
Agent		
Offender		
Criminal		
Snoop		
Lawbreaker		

FAST FINISHERS

Carry out some research and try to find out where some of these terms originally came from.

3 How would you recognise a detective? With your partner, discuss what you think a 'typical' detective might look like, what a detective might wear and how he or she might behave. Write down your ideas and be ready to share your opinions with the class. When explaining your opinions, try to include as much detail as possible. Aim to speak in full sentences and include the word 'because' to justify your ideas.

? PRACTICE QUESTION

Read the extract again. Choose **four** statements below which are **true**. [4 marks]

- Copy out the ones that you think are true.
- Choose a maximum of four true statements.

A The murder victim was called Jefferson Hope. ☐

B It took a long time to arrest the criminal. ☐

C Holmes and the police were so shocked at first that they did not move. ☐

D Lestrade is an inspector involved in the arrest. ☐

E Jefferson Hope doesn't put up any fight when he is being arrested. ☐

F Jefferson Hope badly cut his hands when jumping through the window. ☐

G The prisoner struggled so violently that his hands and feet had to be bound. ☐

H At the end of the extract, the prisoner makes another dash for freedom and escapes. ☐

4 Lamb to the Slaughter

By Roald Dahl

▲ Mary prepares to murder her husband with the frozen leg of lamb

LEARNING OBJECTIVES

⚙ To select evidence purposefully.

⚙ To understand how the writer creates mood and atmosphere.

⚙ To comment on the writer's presentation of characters.

CONTEXT

Roald Dahl (1916–1990) is a famous author of children's books and is probably best known for novels such as *Charlie and the Chocolate Factory*, *Matilda*, *The Twits* and *Fantastic Mr Fox*. However, he also wrote many stories full of suspense for an older audience, with mysterious twists and shocks along the way.

The following extract is taken from the short story 'Lamb to the Slaughter', in which an ordinary housewife, Mary Maloney, has murdered her husband Patrick (a police officer) with a frozen leg of lamb! However, she claims she came home from a shopping trip to find her husband dead. At this point in the story, the investigating officer, Jack Noonan, has arrived to try to solve the murder.

Mary Maloney peeps through the curtains to watch the policemen as they search for the murder weapon.

The search went on. She knew that there were other policemen in the garden all around the house. She could hear their footsteps on the gravel outside, and sometimes she saw a flash of a torch through a chink in the curtains. It began to get late, nearly nine she noticed by the clock on the mantle. The four men searching the rooms seemed to be growing weary, a trifle exasperated.

'Jack,' she said, the next time Sergeant Noonan went by. 'Would you mind giving me a drink?'

'Sure I'll give you a drink. You mean this whisky?'

'Yes please. But just a small one. It might make me feel better.'

He handed her the glass.

Mary asks Sergeant Noonan to bring her a glass of whisky to help calm her down. She behaves in a kind and friendly way by offering the sergeant a drink as well.

'Why don't you have one yourself,' she said. 'You must be awfully tired. Please do. You've been very good to me.'

'Well,' he answered. 'It's not strictly allowed, but I might take just a drop to keep me going.'

One by one the others came in and were persuaded to take a little nip of whisky. They stood around rather awkwardly with the drinks in their hands, uncomfortable in her presence, trying to say consoling things to her. Sergeant Noonan wandered into the kitchen, came out quickly and said, 'Look, Mrs Maloney. You know that oven of yours is still on, and the meat still inside.'

> The Sergeant notices that Mary has left meat cooking in the oven and she asks him to turn it off.

'Oh dear me!' she cried. 'So it is!'

'I better turn it off for you, hadn't I?'

'Will you do that, Jack? Thank you so much.'

When the sergeant returned the second time, she looked at him with her large, dark tearful eyes. 'Jack Noonan,' she said.

'Yes?'

'Would you do me a small favour – you and these others?'

'We can try, Mrs Maloney.'

'Well,' she said. 'Here you all are, and good friends of dear Patrick's too, and helping to catch the man who killed him. You must be terribly hungry by now because it's long past your suppertime, and I know Patrick would never forgive me, God bless his soul, if I allowed you to remain in his house without offering you decent hospitality. Why don't you eat up that lamb that's in the oven. It'll be cooked just right by now.'

> Mary Maloney asks the policemen if they would do her a favour and eat the cooked leg of lamb as she is too emotional and uncomfortable to eat anything that she had prepared for her now-dead husband.

'Wouldn't dream of it,' Sergeant Noonan said.

'Please,' she begged. 'Please eat it. Personally I couldn't touch a thing, certainly not what's been in the house when he was here. But it's all right for you. It'd be a favour to me if you'd eat it up. Then you can go on with your work again afterwards.'

> At first, the policemen are reluctant and feel a bit uncomfortable, but Mary keeps insisting. This creates quite an awkward atmosphere.

There was a good deal of hesitating among the four policemen, but they were clearly hungry, and in the end they were persuaded to go into the kitchen and help themselves. The woman stayed where she was, listening to them speaking among themselves, their voices thick and sloppy because their mouths were full of meat.

'Have some more, Charlie?'

'No. Better not finish it.'

'She wants us to finish it. She said so. Be doing her a favour.'

'Okay then. Give me some more.'

'That's the hell of a big club the guy must've used to hit poor Patrick,' one of them was saying. 'The doc says his skull was smashed all to pieces just like from a sledgehammer.'

> As they are eating and enjoying the meal, the policemen discuss what happened to Mary's husband and are surprised that they haven't been able to find the murder weapon.

'That's why it ought to be easy to find.'

'Exactly what I say.'

'Whoever did it, they're not going to be carrying a thing like that around with them longer than they need.'

One of them belched.

'Personally, I think it's right here on the premises.'

'Probably right under our very noses. What you think, Jack?'

And in the other room, Mary Maloney began to giggle.

> As Mary is in the next room listening to this conversation, she begins to giggle at the irony of the situation – the policemen are actually eating the murder weapon! Mary knows that she has deceived the police and got away with murder!

GLOSSARY

Chink: gap

Mantle: mantelpiece above the fire

Weary: tired

Trifle exasperated: a bit frustrated and fed up

Nip: drop

Consoling: comforting

Hospitality: welcome

Belched: burped

Premises: building/house

SKILLS FOCUS

✔ Understand how writers create effect through language.

✔ Produce a lively written account in role as a character.

✔ Comment on writers' presentation of characters, using appropriate references from texts.

LOOK CLOSER

1. Mary Maloney calls Sergeant Noonan by his first name, Jack, three times in the extract. Explain why you think she repeats his name.

2. Mary is a crafty character who has planned how she can manipulate the policemen. How does the writer use language to create this impression of her? Complete a copy of this table to help you organise your ideas and then write your answer in a paragraph.

Evidence from the text	Impression of Mary
'It might make me feel better.'	This implies that Mary is …
'You've been very good to me.'	This creates the idea that …
'Will you do that, Jack? Thank you so much.'	
'her large, dark tearful eyes'	
'dear Patrick'	

3. When discussing the case, the policemen describe Patrick's injuries as: 'his skull was smashed all to pieces just like from a sledgehammer'. What do these details suggest about the character of Mary? How would this impression be different from Jack Noonan's view of her?

4. Mary is able to deceive the policemen quite easily. What impression does Roald Dahl create of the policemen? Complete a copy of the table below and then write your answer in a paragraph.

Evidence from the text	Impression of the policemen
'seemed to be growing weary'	This makes the reader think that …
'I might take just a drop to keep me going'	
'They stood around rather awkwardly'	
'One of them belched.'	
'Probably right under our very noses.'	

NOW TRY THIS

1 Imagine you are Mary Maloney. Write an entry in your diary describing your thoughts and feelings about what happens when the police arrive at your house to investigate the murder of your husband. Remember the following points:

- ✪ Write in first person narrative.
- ✪ Think about Mary's opinion of the police.
- ✪ Write in full sentences and paragraphs.

You can use this opening sentence or one of your own, if you prefer:

> *I can't believe that I have actually got away with murder!*

2 (a) What notes do you think Sergeant Jack Noonan would have written down about this case? Write the notes that you think he would have made.

(b) Would these notes be different from the report he would write up for the Chief Inspector? Explain the difference and then write the report Sergeant Noonan would give to his Chief Inspector. You might want to use this opening sentence for your report:

> *On Friday 13 May 2019, I received a call to attend an incident at the house of Patrick Maloney, a colleague and police officer.*

FAST FINISHERS

A lot of dialogue is used in this extract but Roald Dahl does not often use the word 'said'. With a partner, make a list of synonyms or alternative verbs for the word 'said' that would indicate how the person speaking is feeling. Have a competition with other groups in the class to see who can think of the most verbs! Here are a few examples to begin with:

- ✪ Bellowed
- ✪ Groaned
- ✪ Sobbed

3 Using the following details, make up a murder whodunit story line with your partner by inventing possible suspects and motives. Discuss your ideas, produce your plan and present your whodunit to the rest of the class.

- ✪ Place – a manor house in the English countryside
- ✪ Victim – Lord Sotherby, the owner of the manor
- ✪ Weapon – a rope
- ✪ Body found – in the library

❓ PRACTICE QUESTION

Read the story again. How has Roald Dahl structured the extract to interest you as a reader? Think about what happens at the beginning, what happens in the middle and whether this is a turning point, and then what happens at the end. Write three paragraphs.

[8 marks]

5 The Adventure of the Final Problem

By Arthur Conan Doyle

▲ Holmes and Moriarty fall to their deaths at Reichenbach Falls

LEARNING OBJECTIVES

- To recognise implicit ideas in a text.
- To explore the writer's techniques.
- To comment on the writer's presentation of characters.

CONTEXT

Many detectives have an arch enemy or master criminal to defeat and capture. 'The Adventure of the Final Problem' is a short story about the fictional detective Sherlock Holmes. In this story, there is no case for Holmes to solve; instead it tells the story of Holmes' final showdown with his arch enemy, the notorious Professor Moriarty. At the end of the story, Holmes and Moriarty fall to their deaths at Reichenbach Falls, after a tense fight. Holmes sacrifices his life to protect the world from the evil of Moriarty.

In the following extract, Sherlock Holmes is describing the character of Professor Moriarty to Dr Watson.

Moriarty is described as clever and a good organiser who doesn't commit the crimes himself but encourages others to do his dirty work for him.

Holmes is appalled at how evil Moriarty is, yet, at the same time, he is impressed by his intelligence and ability.

'He is the Napoleon of crime, Watson. He is the organiser of half that is evil and of nearly all that is undetected in this great city. He is a genius, a philosopher, an abstract thinker. He has a brain of the first order. He sits motionless, like a spider in the centre of its web, but that web has a thousand radiations, and he knows well every quiver of each of them. He does little himself. He only plans. But his agents are numerous and splendidly organised. Is there a crime to be done, a paper to be abstracted, we will say, a house to be rifled, a man to be removed – the word is passed to the Professor, the matter is organised and carried out. The agent may be caught. In that case, money is found for his bail or his defence. But the central power which uses the agent is never caught – never so much as suspected. This was the organisation which I deduced, Watson, and which I devoted my whole energy to exposing and breaking up.

I had met an antagonist who was my intellectual equal. My horror at his crimes was lost in my admiration at his skill. But, at last, he made a trip – only a little, little trip – but it was more than he could afford, when I was so close upon him. I had my chance, and, starting from that point, I have woven my net round him until now it is all

Holmes describes Moriarty as an evil criminal genius who has not yet been caught.

Moriarty has managed to get away with all the crimes he has been connected with.

Moriarty has finally made a mistake and Holmes is ready to set a trap for him.

ready to close. In three days, that is to say on Monday next, matters will be ripe, and the Professor, with all the principal members of his gang, will be in the hands of the police. Then will come the greatest criminal trial of the century, the clearing up of over 40 mysteries and the rope for all of them – but if we move at all prematurely, you understand, they may slip out of our hands even at the last moment.

Now, if I could have done this without the knowledge of Professor Moriarty, all would have been well. But he was too wily for that … I was sitting in my room thinking the matter over, when the door opened and Professor Moriarty stood before me …

His appearance was quite familiar to me. He is extremely tall and thin, his forehead domes out in a white curve, and his two eyes are deeply sunken in his head. He is clean-shaven, pale, and ascetic-looking, retaining something of the professor in his features. His shoulders are rounded from much study, and his face protrudes forward, and is for ever slowly oscillating from side to side in a curiously reptilian fashion.

> Holmes is preparing for Moriarty and his gang to be caught and sentenced to death.

> Holmes is taken by surprise as Moriarty enters his sitting room.

GLOSSARY

Napoleon of crime: criminal mastermind
Undetected: undiscovered
Philosopher: thinker
Abstract thinker: someone who thinks 'outside the box'
Radiations: scatterings
Abstracted: removed
Rifled: searched through
Deduced: guessed or worked out
Antagonist: enemy
Prematurely: before the right time
Wily: crafty
Ascetic: disciplined
Oscillating: moving

SKILLS FOCUS

✔ Understand how writers create effect through language.
✔ Recognise and comment on the effect of writers' techniques, including use of figurative language.
✔ Produce clear and lively written work.

LOOK CLOSER

1 Read this description of Moriarty:

> He sits motionless, like a spider in the centre of its web, but that web has a thousand radiations, and he knows well every quiver of each of them.

The writer has used a simile to describe him. Explain what this image suggests about Moriarty. Do you think this gives the reader a positive or negative impression of him?

2 Read the final paragraph again. How does the writer use language to describe the appearance of Moriarty? Copy and complete the table to help you organise your ideas and then write your answer in a paragraph.

Evidence from the text	Effect on the reader
'extremely tall and thin'	This makes the reader think that …
'forehead domes out in a white curve'	This suggests that …
'eyes are deeply sunken in his head'	
'His shoulders are rounded from much study'	
'oscillating … in a curiously reptilian fashion'	

3 How many crimes does Sherlock Holmes think that Moriarty has been involved in?

4 When describing his plan to capture Moriarty, Sherlock Holmes states, 'I have woven my net round him until now it is all ready to close.' Explain what he means here and write about the effect of this image.

NOW TRY THIS

1 Create your own villain or master criminal. Your character can be from any period in time. You can use a copy of the table below to help you:

Name of villain	
Appearance Face Body Features	
Clothes	
Accessories	
Personality	
Any special talent or skill?	
What makes him or her a villain?	
Any other details	

2 Imagine that a detective apprehends your criminal committing a crime. The criminal tries to escape. Write three paragraphs describing the confrontation and the chase that follows. Remember to:

- ✪ make your writing sound tense and dramatic
- ✪ use exciting and dynamic verbs and adverbs
- ✪ use dialogue to add to the drama of the situation.

You might want to start with this line:

- ✪ A tall, dark shadow loomed over him and at once he knew he had been caught!

FAST FINISHERS

Draw and label a picture of your villain.

3 With a partner, think about the following statement:
'Moriarty is nothing more than a common criminal.'
Work together and discuss evidence that agrees or disagrees with this viewpoint. You can use a table like this to arrange your points.

Agrees with statement	Disagrees with statement
He has organised many criminal activities.	Sherlock Holmes admires his intelligence.

Decide which viewpoint you agree with more and be prepared to deliver your opinions to the class.

❓ PRACTICE QUESTION

Read the extract again. How does the writer use language to show the reader that Moriarty is evil? Write at least three paragraphs in response. Here are some sentence starters to help you with your first paragraph:

- ✪ The first way that the writer uses language to show us that Moriarty is evil is …
- ✪ The writer uses the words …
- ✪ This suggests that …   [8 marks]

6 The No. 1 Ladies' Detective Agency

By Alexander McCall Smith

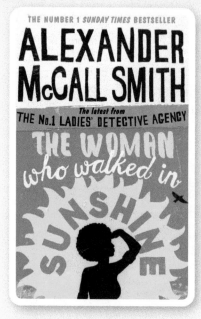

THE NUMBER 1 *SUNDAY TIMES* BESTSELLER

ALEXANDER McCALL SMITH

The latest from THE No.1 LADIES' DETECTIVE AGENCY

THE WOMAN who walked in SUNSHINE

▲ Another case for Mma Ramotswe

LEARNING OBJECTIVES

- To recognise implicit and explicit ideas in a text.
- To comment on the writer's presentation of characters.
- To understand social and historical context.

CONTEXT

The No. 1 Ladies' Detective Agency is the first book in a series of novels by Alexander McCall Smith, set in Botswana in Africa. The main character is Mma Precious Ramotswe who sets up a detective agency with money from the sale of herds of cattle left to her in her father's will. The term Mma is used as a term of respect and means the same as the title Mrs. The mysteries that Mma Ramotswe solves are not serious or sinister crimes, but they usually give the reader a glimpse into human nature and behaviour.

The following extract describes Mma Ramotswe and her detective agency office.

Mma Ramotswe had a detective agency in Africa, at the foot of Kgale Hill. These were its assets: a tiny white van, two desks, two chairs, a telephone and an old typewriter. Then there was a teapot, in which Mma Ramotswe – the only lady private detective in Botswana – brewed redbush tea. And three mugs – one for herself, one for her secretary and one for the client. What else does a detective agency really need? Detective agencies rely on human intuition and intelligence, both of which Mma Ramotswe had in abundance …

She had a sign painted in bright colours, which was then set up just off the Lobatse Road, on the edge of town, pointing to the small building she had purchased.

> *The no 1 ladies' detective agency. For all confidential matters and enquiries.*
>
> *Satisfaction guaranteed for all parties. Under personal management.*

There was considerable public interest in the setting up of her agency. There was an interview on Radio Botswana, in which she thought she was rather rudely pressed to reveal her qualifications, and a rather more satisfactory article in *The Botswana News*,

There are very few possessions or home comforts in the office. Mma Ramotswe only has things that are necessary to do her job and doesn't have any luxuries or modern items.

The detective agency is at the bottom of the Kgale Hill in Botswana. It would have been unusual for there to be a female detective agency in the 1980s and 1990s.

This is the sign that Mma Ramotswe uses to advertise the agency. The adjective 'confidential' would persuade people that they could trust Mma Ramotswe.

Mma Ramotswe has quite a lot of publicity because she has set up the first ladies' detective agency in Botswana.

Mma Ramotswe is very proud of what people have written about her and she wants all of her clients to see the article.

In Mma Ramotswe's experience, people are happy to speak to detectives as it makes them feel special and important.

The cases she deals with are about the ordinary, day-to-day concerns of local people – there are no sensational cases.

She has a good understanding of human nature and how people behave.

which drew attention to the fact that she was the only lady private detective in the country. This article was cut out, copied and placed prominently on a small board beside the front door of the agency.

After a slow start she was rather surprised to find that her services were in considerable demand. She was consulted about missing husbands, about the creditworthiness of potential business partners and about suspected fraud by employees. In almost every case, she was able to come up with at least some information for the client; when she could not, she waived her fee, which meant that virtually nobody who consulted her was dissatisfied. People in Botswana liked to talk, she discovered, and the mere mention of the fact that she was a private detective would let loose a positive outpouring of information on all sorts of subjects. It flattered people, she concluded, to be approached by a private detective, and this effectively loosened their tongues.

This happened with Happy Bapetsi, one of her earlier clients. Poor Happy! 'I used to have a happy life,' said Happy Bapetsi. 'A very happy life. Then this thing happened and I can't say that any more.'

Mma Ramotswe watched her client as she sipped her bush tea. Everything you wanted to know about a person was written in the face, she believed. It's not that she believed that the shape of the head was what counted – even if there were many who still clung to that belief; it was more a question of taking care to scrutinise the lines and the general look. And the eyes, of course; they were very important. The eyes allowed you to see right into a person, to penetrate their very essence, and that was why people with something to hide wore sunglasses indoors. They were the ones you had to watch very carefully …

GLOSSARY

Assets: belongings or possessions

Intuition: gut feeling

In abundance: a lot of

Purchased: bought

Confidential: private

Pressed: pressurised

Prominently: in clear view

Fraud: theft

Waived her fee: did not charge

Virtually nobody: hardly anyone

Outpouring: rush of words

Concluded: decided

Loosened their tongues: encouraged them to talk

Scrutinise: examine or inspect

Penetrate: look through

Essence: soul

SKILLS FOCUS

✔ Understand how writers create effect through language.

✔ Use different types of questions for different purposes.

✔ Hold a lively discussion.

▲ 'An old typewriter'

LOOK CLOSER

1. Write down four facts you have found out about the No. 1 Ladies' Detective Agency.

2. Look closely again at the sign advertising the detective agency.

> The no 1 ladies' detective agency. For all confidential matters and enquiries.
> Satisfaction guaranteed for all parties. Under personal management.

Which words do you think would persuade people to use the agency? Explain why you think these words would be persuasive.

3. Mma Ramotswe's detective agency is a successful one. How does the writer use language to suggest this? Copy and complete the table and then write your answer in a paragraph.

Evidence from the text	Effect on the reader
'Detective agencies rely on human intuition and intelligence, both of which Mma Ramotswe had in abundance'	This creates the effect that …
'There was considerable public interest'	
'her services were in considerable demand.'	
'In almost every case, she was able to come up with at least some information for the client'	
'She was consulted about missing husbands, about the creditworthiness of potential business partners and about suspected fraud by employees'	
'one of her earlier clients'	

4. In Mma Ramotswe's experience, how do people behave when they meet a detective? Refer to words and evidence from the text to support your answer.

NOW TRY THIS

1. In the extract, Happy Bapetsi says to Mma Ramotswe, 'I used to have a happy life … A very happy life. Then this thing happened and I can't say that any more.' What do you think has happened? Imagine you are Happy. Write an account of what you think has occurred and how you persuade Mma Ramotswe to help you.

   ✪ Remember to write in full sentences and clear paragraphs.

   ✪ Write in first person narrative.

   ✪ Think about any persuasive words and techniques you would use to make sure Mma Ramotswe would help you.

2 At the start of the extract, there is a description of Mma Ramotswe's office and the sign she has placed outside to attract clients.

(a) Imagine you are a detective setting up your own agency. Think of a name for your agency and the type of detective you will be.

(b) Design your office and decide what possessions and equipment you will need. Draw a diagram of your office and explain why each item is needed.

(c) Finally, write a sign or an advertisement that will attract potential clients and persuade them to use your services.

FAST FINISHERS

Mma Ramotswe says that people are often ready to speak to detectives. If you want people or witnesses to give you information, you need to think carefully about the type of questions you ask them. For example, 'closed' questions will only give you a brief answer and will not be very useful to you. However, 'open' questions will give the witness more opportunity to describe what happened.

Decide which of the following questions are 'closed' questions or 'open' questions.

A Did you see what happened?

B What happened?

C What was the suspect wearing?

D How was the suspect behaving?

E Did the suspect act suspiciously?

Make up another two 'closed' questions and two 'open' questions of your own.

3 What advice do you think would be helpful to a person who is thinking of setting up a detective agency? With a partner, produce a list of ten Dos and Don'ts for becoming a successful detective agency. Be prepared to explain your list to the class. Here is one to start you off:

(1) Do make sure that your office is in a location that people can find easily.

❓ PRACTICE QUESTION

Read the extract again. How does the writer use language to show the reader that Mma Ramotswe is a good detective? (You might want to look back at the Look Closer section for ideas.) Write at least three paragraphs in response. Here are some sentence starters to help you with your first paragraph:

✿ The first way that the writer uses language to show us that Mma Ramotswe is a good detective is by ...

✿ The writer uses the words ...

✿ This suggests that ...   [8 marks]

7 The Mysterious Affair at Styles

By Agatha Christie

▲ Hercule Poirot as he investigates one of his many cases

LEARNING OBJECTIVES

- To recognise implicit ideas in a text.
- To understand how the writer creates mood and atmosphere.
- To comment on the writer's presentation of characters.

CONTEXT

Agatha Christie (1890–1976) is well known for her mystery stories and the creation of two famous fictional detectives, Miss Marple and Hercule Poirot. Many of her stories and novels have been made into films or television series. Some of her most famous novels include *Murder on the Orient Express*, *Death on the Nile* and *The ABC Murders*. Hercule Poirot, the Belgian detective renowned for his moustache and intelligence, first appeared in the novel *The Mysterious Affair at Styles*. The following extract is taken from this novel as Poirot is inspecting a suspected crime scene with Captain Hastings, who is narrating the events.

Poirot locked the door on the inside, and proceeded to a minute inspection of the room. He darted from one object to the other with the agility of a grasshopper. I remained by the door, fearing to obliterate any clues …

A small purple despatch-case, with a key in the lock, on the writing-table, engaged his attention for some time. He took out the key from the lock, and passed it to me to inspect. I saw nothing peculiar, however. It was an ordinary key of the Yale type, with a bit of twisted wire through the handle.

Next, he examined the framework of the door we had broken in, assuring himself that the bolt had really been shot. Then he went to the door opposite leading into Cynthia's room. That door was also bolted, as I had stated. However, he went to the length of unbolting it, and opening and shutting it several times; this he did with the utmost precaution against making any noise. Suddenly something in the bolt itself seemed to rivet his attention. He examined it carefully, and then, nimbly whipping out a pair of small forceps from his case, he drew out some minute particle which he carefully sealed up in a tiny envelope.

On the chest of drawers there was a tray with a spirit lamp and a small saucepan on it. A small quantity of a dark fluid remained in the saucepan, and an empty cup and saucer that had been drunk out of stood near it.

I wondered how I could have been so unobservant as to overlook this. Here was a clue worth having. Poirot delicately dipped his finger into liquid, and tasted it gingerly. He made a grimace.

Poirot examines objects carefully and quickly in the room which is a possible crime scene.

Poirot is interested in a key, although Hastings doesn't seem very interested in it.

Poirot begins opening and closing the door to check how much noise it makes. He then notices a small piece of evidence that he carefully puts inside an envelope to examine later.

'Coco – with – I think – rum in it.'

> Poirot tastes the remains of a liquid in the cup – coco with some alcohol: rum.

He passed on to the debris on the floor, where the table by the bed had been overturned. A reading-lamp, some books, matches, a bunch of keys, and the crushed fragments of a coffee-cup lay scattered about.

'Ah, this is curious,' said Poirot.

'I must confess that I see nothing particularly curious about it.'

> Captain Hastings doesn't understand why this is important or why Poirot is interested in it.

'You do not? Observe the lamp – the chimney is broken in two places; they lie there as they fell. But see, the coffee-cup is absolutely smashed to powder.'

'Well,' I said wearily, 'I suppose someone must have stepped on it.'

'Exactly,' said Poirot, in an odd voice. 'Someone stepped on it.'

> Poirot speaks decisively as he can see the case beginning to come together as they collect evidence.

He rose from his knees, and walked slowly across to the mantelpiece, where he stood abstractedly fingering the ornaments, and straightening them – a trick of his when he was agitated.

'Mon ami,' he said, turning to me, 'somebody stepped on that cup, grinding it to powder, and the reason they did so was either because it contained strychnine or – which is far more serious – because it did not contain strychnine!'

> Tension builds in the extract as Poirot mentions the possibility of poison.

I made no reply. I was bewildered, but I knew that it was no good asking him to explain. In a moment or two he roused himself, and went on with his investigations. He picked up the bunch of keys from the floor, and twirling them round in his fingers finally selected one, very bright and shining, which he tried in the lock of the purple despatch-case. It fitted, and he opened the box, but after a moment's hesitation, closed and relocked it, and slipped the bunch of keys, as well as the key that had originally stood in the lock, into his own pocket.

> Poirot picks up a bunch of keys and eventually puts them in his pocket, suggesting they will be important to the case later.

GLOSSARY

Minute: precise

Obliterate: destroy

Engaged: caught

Utmost precaution: greatest care

Rivet his attention: grab his attention

Forceps: pliers

Overlook: miss or not notice

Gingerly: carefully

Grimace: an expression of disgust on the face

Debris: rubbish

Abstractedly: thoughtfully or distractedly

Agitated: anxious

Mon ami: 'my friend'

Strychnine: poison

Bewildered: confused

SKILLS FOCUS

✔ Select evidence purposefully.

✔ Recognise and comment on the effect of writers' techniques, including use of figurative language.

✔ Listen and respond appropriately to spoken language.

LOOK CLOSER

1 Read this description of Poirot:

> He darted from one object to the other with the agility of a grasshopper.

The writer has used an interesting image to describe him. Explain what this image suggests about Poirot. What does the verb 'dart' suggest about his movements?

2 Poirot and Hastings are very different characters in the way they behave. How does Agatha Christie use language to show the differences between them? Fill in a copy of this table to organise your ideas and then write your answer.

Poirot	Hastings	Difference between Poirot and Hastings
'minute inspection'	'fearing to obliterate any clues'	The words '_____' suggest that … Poirot is … However, the words '_____' suggest Hastings is …
'engaged his attention'	'I saw nothing peculiar'	
'he examined it carefully'	'how I could have been so unobservant as to overlook this'	
'"Ah, this is curious," said Poirot.'	'"I must confess that I see nothing particularly curious about it."'	

3 In the extract, the writer uses dashes (–) in some places. Find examples of where the writer does this and explain what effect the dashes create.

4 List four things that catch Poirot's attention in the extract.

NOW TRY THIS

1 Poirot is very observant and is skilful at solving puzzling situations and mysteries. Write an account of a time when you solved a confusing or mysterious situation, or a time when something unexpected happened to you. Remember to:

- ✪ use sentences and paragraphs
- ✪ use dialogue to make the situation interesting and vivid
- ✪ use adjectives and images to interest the reader.

2 The writer uses an animal image to describe one of Poirot's characteristics. How would you describe yourself and your qualities? Complete the following sentences – the first one has been done as an example:

- ✪ If I were an animal, I would be a tiger because I am energetic and can be fierce.
- ✪ If I were a piece of furniture, I would be a _____ because ...
- ✪ If I were an animal, I would be a _____ because ...
- ✪ If I were a colour, I would be _____ because ...
- ✪ If I were an emotion, I would be _____ because ...
- ✪ If I were a country, I would be _____ because ...
- ✪ If I were the weather, I would be _____ because ...
- ✪ If I were a season, I would be _____ because ...

FAST FINISHERS

- ✪ Choose another four examples of your own.
- ✪ On a large piece of paper, create your own character wall about yourself using these descriptions and anything else you would like to add. Illustrate your descriptions or cut out pictures from magazines to go on your character wall.

3 Hastings doesn't understand the importance of what Poirot has found, so Poirot has to explain carefully what he means. Imagine that your partner has been transported to your class from hundreds of years ago and doesn't understand what some modern day items are. Explain to your partner what the following items are and what they are used for:

- ✪ a biro
- ✪ a mobile phone
- ✪ headphones
- ✪ trainers.

4 Think of a day-to-day, modern item and describe it to your partner without revealing what it is. Can your partner guess what you are describing? Be careful not to mention the name of the item!

❓ PRACTICE QUESTION

Read the extract again. How does the writer use language to create a positive impression of Poirot? Write at least three paragraphs in response. Here are some sentence starters to help you with your first paragraph:

- ✪ The first way that the writer uses language to create a positive impression of Poirot is ...
- ✪ The writer uses the words ...
- ✪ This makes the reader think that ... [8 marks]

▲ Edgar Allan Poe

LEARNING OBJECTIVES

⊛ To recognise implicit and explicit ideas in a text.

⊛ To explore writers' techniques.

⊛ To comment on the writer's creation of character and relationships.

CONTEXT

Edgar Allan Poe (1809–1849) was an American writer of horror and mystery stories. It is generally believed that he created the genre of detective fiction and that's why he was called 'the father of the detective story'. He produced the first fictional detective character, Auguste Dupin, which in turn inspired the creation of Sherlock Holmes and Hercule Poirot. The short story 'The Murders in the Rue Morgue' is considered to be the first detective story and the following extract is taken from this story. It is written from the viewpoint of an unnamed narrator, Dupin's friend.

The narrator gives information about Dupin's background and his great love of books.

Dupin was the last member of a well-known family, a family which had once been rich and famous; he himself, however, was far from rich. He cared little about money. He had enough to buy the most necessary things of life – and a few books; he did not trouble himself about the rest. Just books. With books he was happy.

We first met when we were both trying to find the same book. As it was a book which few had ever heard of, this chance brought us together in an old bookstore. Later we met again in the same store. Then again in another bookstore. Soon we began to talk.

Dupin and the narrator share an interest in books and they strike up a conversation as they keep bumping into each other in bookshops.

I was deeply interested in the family history he told me. I was surprised, too, at how much and how widely he had read; more important, the force of his busy mind was like a bright light in my soul. I felt that the friendship of such a man would be for me riches without price. I therefore told him of my feelings toward him, and he agreed to come and live with me. He would have, I thought, the joy of using my many fine books. And I would have the pleasure of having someone with me, for I was not happy alone.

As a result of their shared passion for books, and because the narrator does not like living alone, he invites Dupin to move in with him as a friend.

We passed the days reading, writing and talking. But Dupin was a lover of the night, and at night, often with only the light of the stars to show us the way, we walked the streets of Paris, sometimes talking, sometimes quiet, always thinking.

I soon noticed a special reasoning power he had, an unusual reasoning power. Using it gave him great pleasure. He told me once, with a soft and quiet laugh, that most men have windows over their hearts; through these he could see into their souls. Then, he surprised me by telling what he knew about my own soul; and I found that he knew things about me that I had thought only I could possibly know. His manner at these moments was cold and distant. His eyes looked empty and far away, and his voice became high and nervous. At such times it seemed to me that I saw not just Dupin, but two Dupins – one who coldly put things together, and another who just as coldly took them apart.

The narrator notices a special talent that Dupin has for understanding and working things out.

The narrator is in awe of how perceptive Dupin is and how he has the ability to look deep inside a person's thoughts. This is a really useful skill when solving crimes!

One night we were walking down one of Paris's long and dirty streets. Both of us were busy with our thoughts. Neither had spoken for perhaps fifteen minutes. It seemed as if we had each forgotten that the other was there, at his side. I soon learned that Dupin had not forgotten me, however. Suddenly he said: 'You're right. He is a very little fellow, that's true, and he would be more successful if he acted in lighter, less serious plays.'

While Dupin and the narrator are going for a walk one evening, Dupin turns to the narrator and makes a comment about an actor they have recently seen.

'Yes, there can be no doubt of that!' I said. At first I saw nothing strange in this. Dupin had agreed with me, with my own thoughts. This, of course, seemed to me quite natural. For a few seconds I continued walking, and thinking; but suddenly I realised that Dupin had agreed with something which was only a thought. I had not spoken a single word. I stopped walking and turned to my friend. 'Dupin,' I said. 'Dupin, this is beyond my understanding. How could you know that I was thinking of …?'

The narrator suddenly realises that he has not spoken an opinion, but Dupin has been able to read his mind and know what he is thinking.

GLOSSARY

Riches: wealth

Passed: spent

Reasoning: understanding

SKILLS FOCUS

✔ Create a lively description.

✔ Listen and respond appropriately to spoken language.

✔ Comment on writers' presentation of characters, using appropriate references from texts.

LOOK CLOSER

1. List four facts that we find out about Dupin from the extract.

2. In which city do Dupin and the narrator live? Find evidence to support your answer.

3. Dupin tells the narrator that 'most men have windows over their hearts; through these he could see into their souls.' Explain what you think Dupin means by saying this and write about the effect of the image used.

4. Read the first five paragraphs again. How does Poe use language to describe the character of Dupin? Complete a copy of this table to help you organise your ideas and then write your answer in a paragraph.

Evidence from the text	Impressions of Dupin
'He cared little about money'	This gives the impression that ...
'how widely he had read'	
'with a soft and quiet laugh'	
'His manner at these moments was cold and distant.'	
'His eyes looked empty and far away'	
'his voice became high and nervous'	

NOW TRY THIS

1 Dupin and the narrator have a good friendship and share common interests because they met through their love of books. Write a couple of paragraphs describing your best friend and his or her character and personality. What interests do you share? What does your friend mean to you?

2 What qualities, do you think, make a good friend? Design a poster for the Ten Golden Rules of Friendship. Think about how you would present your ideas and the type of language you will use.

FAST FINISHERS

Research the life of Edgar Allan Poe and other detective stories that he wrote. Write a fact file containing all of your information.

3 The narrator is amazed that Dupin seems to be able to read his mind and know what he is thinking. Dupin uses this skill to great effect when he is solving crimes. Imagine you had a special skill that would amaze other people. What would your special skill be? It can be as imaginative and unbelievable as you want!

Discuss your skill with your partner. Be prepared to explain your special skill to the class and persuade them why your skill is useful!

? PRACTICE QUESTION

Read the extract again. How does the writer use language to create an impression of the narrator? Use evidence from the text to support your points. Here are some sentence starters to help you:

- ✪ The first way that the writer uses language to create an impression of the narrator is ...
- ✪ In the extract the writer uses the words ...
- ✪ This suggests that ...   [8 marks]

9 In Search of Sherlock

From an article in *National Geographic* magazine by Shreya Sen Handley, 2 January 2017

▲ Fox Tor Mire on Dartmoor, where *The Hound of the Baskervilles* is set

LEARNING OBJECTIVES

- To be able to retrieve implicit and explicit information.
- To analyse the writer's use of language.
- To listen and respond appropriately to spoken language.

CONTEXT

Shreya Sen Handley is a writer and columnist who also creates travelogues for the magazine *National Geographic*. In this article, she and her husband are travelling around Britain looking for some of the locations made famous by Arthur Conan Doyle in his stories about Sherlock Holmes. Here you can read about their visit to Baskerville Hall and the creepy moor where *The Hound of the Baskervilles* is supposedly set.

The words 'enduring affection' show that the writer and her husband have enjoyed murder mystery stories for a long time.

A simile 'like a large dog' is used to suggest that the mansion is almost scared of the bad weather.

The real Baskerville Hall looks just as sinister and creepy as Conan Doyle's fictitious description in his novel.

At the heart of our shared love of whodunits is an enduring affection for Arthur Conan Doyle's master sleuth. Over the years, we have visited many places connected to Sherlock's adventures, but rarely by design. Like Arthur Conan Doyle, who travelled extensively, setting his stories against the many glorious backdrops this small island has to offer, we enjoy exploring Britain.

That afternoon, we found ourselves driving up a windswept rise, to the dark mass of the mansion atop it, crouched against the lashing wind like a large dog. Conan Doyle is believed to have been a frequent guest of the Baskervilles of Baskerville Hall, built in 1839. On his visits, he learned of the local legend of the hound of the Baskervilles, and scribbling in his journal on nearby Hergest Ridge, he made it his own. But at the request of his friends, he set the story in the faraway southern county of Devon 'to ward off tourists'. On the day we visited, though the sign swinging in the wind said it was a hotel, it had all the atmosphere of Conan Doyle's Baskerville Hall – shuttered, silent, and more than a little sinister. Our encounter with its owner started on an equally ominous note. So baleful was the man's scrutiny, we worried that we were about to become his dog's (a large one by the sounds of it) dinner. Instead,

The writer and her husband have travelled to many places in Britain.

Conan Doyle used the local story of the hound of the Baskervilles for his novel and his fictional detective, Sherlock Holmes. The verb 'scribbling' shows that Conan Doyle was excited about the story.

The writer soon realises that the inhabitants are friendly and she and her husband are invited to dinner.

much to our surprise, we were invited to dinner. And all because I had uttered the magic word, 'Sherlock'.

Not surprisingly, the next year found us in the bleak Devon moors where he had transplanted the Baskerville tale. Keen to experience Holmes and Watson's chase across dark and dangerous Dartmoor, we set out in the gloaming in search of the path they'd taken for that climactic scene. To our delight, at twilight, modern-day Dartmoor looked no different from its whodunit avatar. Our delight didn't last as the terrain got tougher to negotiate. As the darkening sky fused with the black granite of the moors, it wasn't hard to imagine a large, black dog lying in wait for us in the gloom.

Adjectives are used here to create a threatening atmosphere around the scenery of Dartmoor.

The writer and her husband decide that they would prefer a good meal and a warm place to stay instead of walking across the cold moors.

We staggered over rocky ridges known as 'tors', more interested in returning to our warm inn and perfect coastal dinner of smoked haddock with sautéed potatoes, than finding that mythical path. We certainly did not want to stumble upon Great Grimpen Mire, where Stapleton met his end. Luckily for us, it hadn't rained in a few days, and bogs only form when torrents of rain mix with spongy Dartmoor peat. The next morning, after a hearty English breakfast, we resumed our search for Fox Tor Mire on which Conan Doyle based his beastly bog. Driving as close to it as we could, we got a tor-top view of that famous marsh into which you could disappear forever and never look upon another Sherlock setting again.

The writer and her husband end their visit by visiting the peak overlooking the dangerous marsh.

GLOSSARY

Enduring affection: long-lasting love

Sleuth: detective

By design: as a result of a plan

Extensively: a great deal

Atop: on top of

To ward off tourists: to stop tourists visiting the place

Ominous: threatening

Baleful: menacing

Scrutiny: examination

Transplanted: moved

Gloaming: twilight

Avatar: type

Terrain: ground

Negotiate: get through

Stapleton: the criminal in *The Hound of the Baskervilles*

SKILLS FOCUS

✔ Explain how the writer creates mood and atmosphere.

✔ Recognise and comment on the effect of writers' techniques, including use of figurative language.

✔ Comment on writers' presentation of characters, using appropriate references from texts.

LOOK CLOSER

1. The writer uses descriptive language to create atmosphere in the line 'we found ourselves driving up a windswept rise, to the dark mass of the mansion atop it, crouched against the lashing wind like a large dog.' Explain the effect of some of the descriptive words here and decide what sort of atmosphere is created.

2. Read again the description of the hotel in the second paragraph. How does the writer use language and techniques to make the hotel seem unwelcoming? Fill in a copy of this table to organise your ideas and then write your answer in a paragraph.

Evidence from the text	Effect
'the sign swinging in the wind'	This suggests ...
'shuttered, silent and more than a little sinister'	
'ominous note'	
'So baleful was the man's scrutiny'	
'we worried we were about to become his dog's dinner'	

3. The writer uses examples of alliteration in the phrases 'dark and dangerous Dartmoor' and 'beastly bog.' Explain why these phrases are effective.

4. The article has been divided into three paragraphs. Decide on a suitable sub-heading for each paragraph.

NOW TRY THIS

1. The writer has created descriptions of sinister-looking locations. Write your own description of a creepy place. You might want to write about a graveyard, an abandoned old house, an alleyway or a place of your choice.

   Remember to use interesting descriptive techniques such as similes, metaphors, alliteration and verbs to make your writing interesting.

2. A travelogue is a piece of writing about a traveller's experiences of visiting different places. In the extract, Shreya Sen Handley has written about her experiences of travelling in Britain. Write a travelogue as if you were a traveller visiting your home area for the first time.

FAST FINISHERS

Look at these negative descriptions from the passage in the table below. Turn them into more pleasant descriptions by using positive adjectives. The first one has been completed for you.

Negative description	Positive description
'So baleful was the man's scrutiny'	So friendly was the man's expression
'the darkening sky fused with the black granite of the moors'	
'shuttered, silent, and more than a little sinister'	
'it wasn't hard to imagine a large, black dog lying in wait for us in the gloom'	

3 In groups of two or three, create a television advert persuading people to visit the areas that the writer has described. Think about:

- ✪ information about the areas and their connections with Sherlock Holmes
- ✪ reasons why people would want to visit
- ✪ use of persuasive language and techniques.

❓ PRACTICE QUESTION

Read the extract again. Choose **four** statements below which are **true**.   [4 marks]

- ✪ Copy out the ones that you think are true.
- ✪ Choose a maximum of four true statements.

A Baskerville Hall was built in 1939. ☐

B Conan Doyle wrote his journal at Hergest Ridge. ☐

C Conan Doyle changed the location of the Baskerville tale to Scotland. ☐

D Conan Doyle never actually visited Baskerville Hall. ☐

E 'Tor' is a term for a rocky ridge. ☐

F Stapleton died on Great Grimpen Mire. ☐

G The writer had a good English breakfast. ☐

H In his writing, Conan Doyle based his bog on Wolf Tor Mire. ☐

10 'Poirot has been my best friend'

From an interview in the *Telegraph* newspaper where the actor
David Suchet talks to Elizabeth Grice, 30 October 2013

▲ David Suchet as Hercule
Poirot in the final episode

LEARNING OBJECTIVES

✪ To be able to retrieve implicit and explicit information.

✪ To analyse the writer's use of language.

✪ To organise ideas and information.

CONTEXT

David Suchet is an actor who is well known for playing the role of
Hercule Poirot in the television detective series, *Poirot*. He had played
this character for many years and, in this interview, Suchet explains how
he feels to be playing Poirot for the very last time.

The opening
describes Poirot as
a weak and frail
old man who is
clearly suffering
from ill health.

Clumsy, arthritic fingers scrabble at the bedclothes, reaching
uncertainly for something to alleviate the crushing heart pains.
In a moment of deliberate ambiguity, it is not his amyl nitrate
ampoules that Hercule Poirot grasps from the bedside table but a
rosary. The master-sleuth has never seemed more vulnerable.

The sudden frailty of Agatha Christie's famous Belgian detective
is superbly captured by David Suchet, in his last television
appearance as Poirot after 25 years in the role. In 70 episodes,
he has encompassed the whole canon of murder mysteries
featuring Poirot, the defining role of his career and a broadcasting
tour de force. Now, as ITV screens its concluding episodes over the
next three weeks, he's peeling off the extravagant moustache and
laying aside the gold watch chain for good.

Why do you think
Poirot takes hold
of his rosary
instead of his pain
relief tablets?

The role of Poirot
has been the
most important
part that David
Suchet has played
and it is the one
that everyone will
remember him for.

In the final of all, *Curtain: Poirot's Last Case*, Poirot is a wasted
man, immobilised from the waist down but glittering with intent.
The investigator's fussy, waddling walk and dandified appearance
are scarcely missed as Suchet condenses his formidable acting skills
into his character's hollow features. How does he get that lower
eyelid to twitch like a lizard?

In the final
episode, viewers
will be shocked by
the deterioration
in the health
and physical
appearance of
Poirot.

'He's a walking brain, so when he's in the wheelchair, all the
energy is here,' says Suchet, tapping at the little grey cells. 'I cannot
deny it was the hardest day filming of my whole career,' he says.

David Suchet feels sad to be playing the role for the final time, as the character of Poirot has been such a big part of his life for so long.

'Poirot has been my best friend, part of my family, part of my life. I've lived with this man. He's allowed me the career I don't think I would have had without him. He's given me stability in a profession that is insecure.'

Asked on the final day's filming whether he felt sad, he replied with monumental pride:

'People write to me from all over the world telling me how Poirot has seen them through bereavements and illnesses; how he has comforted them because they feel safe with him.'

Since Suchet has played the part for so long, people have become used to him and he feels like a familiar friend.

Suchet has always paid Poirot the compliment of taking him seriously. 'He wasn't aware of his own silliness,' he says. 'He is a pure eccentric and total eccentrics are unaware of their eccentricity.'

It takes about three minutes in Suchet's crisp but genial presence to detect certain Poirot-like traits. Not a hair is out of place. He is ferociously alert. There are papers on the desk in front of him that he neatens from time to time even though no one has touched them.

Just like the character he plays, Suchet is precise and neat in his behaviour.

'I do like order,' he confesses. 'Poirot is a visual man. If he looks on chaos on his desk, he will feel chaotic. Before I start learning lines for a big play, I have to make my desk absolutely clear so my mind is clear. Then I put the play down and start work. I love symmetry. I will go into a room and, if I'm on my own, I will straighten the crooked picture, as he does. I'm also very traditional as a man. I'm not modern and never have been. I think I was born 50 years of age and out of my time. Poirot's definitely out of his time.'

Suchet admits that he has always seemed older than his age and should have been born into another time.

GLOSSARY

Alleviate: ease

Ambiguity: more than one possibility

Amyl nitrate ampoules: pain relieving drugs

Rosary: a string of beads connected with religion

Vulnerable: weak or defenceless

Encompassed: covered

Canon: collection

Defining role: the part he will be best remembered for

Tour de force: performance achieved with great skill

Immobilised: unable to move

Dandified: fashionable

Monumental: enormous

Bereavements: loss of loved ones

Eccentric: a person who behaves differently

Genial: friendly

Traits: characteristics

Symmetry: balance

SKILLS FOCUS

✔ Understand how writers create effect through language.

✔ Recognise and comment on the effect of writers' techniques.

✔ Understand how the writer conveys feelings.

LOOK CLOSER

1 Find four facts that we learn about David Suchet in this interview.

2 Read the first paragraph again. Explain how the writer makes the reader feel sympathy for the character of Poirot. Fill in the details in a copy of this table to organise your ideas and then write your answer in a paragraph.

Example from the text	Effect
'clumsy, arthritic fingers'	The adjectives suggest that Poirot is …
'scrabble at the bedclothes'	The verb implies …
'reaching uncertainly'	
'grasps'	
'vulnerable'	

3 David Suchet says, 'Poirot has been my best friend, part of my family, part of my life. I've lived with this man.' What does Suchet mean when he says this?

4 Read the interview again. How does the writer show that David Suchet is a good actor? Fill in a copy of the table with evidence from the text to organise your ideas. Some evidence has been included to help you, but you need to track through the interview to find more examples. Write your answer in two paragraphs.

Evidence from the interview	Effect
'superbly captured'	The adverb creates the impression that …
'encompassed the whole canon of murder mysteries'	
'formidable acting skills'	

NOW TRY THIS

1 In the interview, interesting adjectives, verbs and adverbs are used to create a vivid impression of Poirot's old age and frailty. Write a short description of an old person using adjectives, verbs and figurative language to create effect. Think about:

- ❂ appearance
- ❂ movement
- ❂ speech
- ❂ clothing.

2 Based on your description in the previous question, write a contrasting description of the person when he or she was younger.

FAST FINISHERS

Look again at these phrases used in the interview.

- ❂ 'How does he get that lower eyelid to twitch like a lizard?'
- ❂ 'waddling walk'
- ❂ 'He's a walking brain'

Decide what technique is used in each quotation, and explain the effect of each one.

3 With a partner, research the life of a famous actor or singer of your choice.
Imagine you have been given the opportunity to interview this celebrity for a magazine. What questions would you ask the celebrity? What answers would he or she give to your questions?

With your partner, be prepared to act out the interview in front of the class.

❓ PRACTICE QUESTION

What impressions does the interview give of David Suchet? Here are some sentence starters to help you:

- ❂ We have the impression that David Suchet is ...
- ❂ David Suchet says ... and this suggests that ...
- ❂ David Suchet is presented as ...   [8 marks]

11 Jonathan Creek

From an article in the *Guardian* newspaper by Natalie Haynes, 27 November 2012

▲ Jonathan Creek, the unconventional, modern-day detective, with his sidekick, Maddy Magellan

LEARNING OBJECTIVES

- To distinguish the main ideas in a text.
- To be able to retrieve implicit and explicit information.
- To organise ideas and information.

CONTEXT

Natalie Haynes, a British broadcaster and writer, compiled a series of blogs/articles for the *Guardian* newspaper in which she wrote about her top 25 TV detectives. The following article is about the television detective series *Jonathan Creek,* in which the actor and comedian Alan Davies plays the title character.

The magician-turned-sleuth is a modern-day Victorian gentleman detective – more about solving seemingly impossible puzzles than catching criminals.

> An introduction to the article describing the television detective Jonathan Creek.

When Jonathan Creek first appeared in 1997, it was like going back in time. The locked-room mystery was a Victorian crime staple: Edgar Allan Poe and Wilkie Collins were its earliest proponents, and the form was then refined in the early part of the 20th century by the labyrinthine brain of John Dickson Carr. His 'impossible crime' novel, *The Hollow Man*, is still one of the twistiest murder mysteries I have ever read.

> The writer shows similarities between the mysteries solved by Jonathan Creek and the puzzling cases of earlier fictional detectives.

But as the murder mystery morphed into the detective novel – where the key appeal is the appearance of the same detective to solve each crime, rather than the unguessable tricksiness of the murder – the locked room mystery fell out of fashion. Even more so with the recent unstoppable rise of the fictional serial killer: it seems we no longer want an impossible crime, we want an unimaginable one. Well, I don't.

> The writer shows how the interests of the public have changed over time and how mystery stories have become detective stories with a different sort of focus.

I find I can't read 'What's the worst thing in the world?' fiction anymore. Call me a sap if you must, but it is just too nasty for me.

> What impression do we have of the writer when she describes herself as a 'sap'?

Which isn't to say that Jonathan Creek isn't nasty at times: there are some genuinely horrible murders in the mix (*The Grinning Man* is probably the ickiest for me, but take your pick). But at its heart, Jonathan Creek is trying to baffle its audience rather than leaving it too afraid to leave the house. Also, if you're going to sleep in a haunted attic from which seven people have disappeared without trace, don't come crying to me when … well, you'll be in no position to cry, will you?

> The cases of Jonathan Creek are supposed to intrigue and confuse the audience, instead of frightening them, unlike many current detective series.

Jonathan is a pleasingly unlikely detective: half genius, half sheepdog, he makes his living **devising** magic tricks for his boss, magician Adam Klaus (Anthony Head, until Buffy made him a better offer, and Stuart Milligan took over and made the part his own).

Jonathan is the grownup version of every nerdy boy who practises a card trick for two solid days before using it to baffle everyone he knows. He's soft-hearted (those kittens do very well out of him in *The Omega Man*), though he can be grouchy and resistant to getting involved in the whole crime-solving affair.

He's brought into his first case by investigative journalist Maddy Magellan (Caroline Quentin), who does only a limited amount of investigating herself. Rather, she spends **the bulk of** her time saying, 'Honestly, Jonathan,' in an increasingly **shrewish** manner. It's worth noting that Jonathan becomes much grumpier after Magellan hoofs off to America, and while that may be because he misses her, I think it's more likely to be the case that there simply wasn't the space for any more stroppiness when Maddy was around.

The role of a detective is to restore order to the world. When someone is murdered in a detective novel or programme, society is thrown into **upheaval**: everyone is under suspicion, secrets are revealed, no one knows who to trust. Worst of all, there's a cold-blooded killer walking around, pretending to be innocent. The detective steps in and re-imposes order on the chaos left behind by the murder.

But Jonathan Creek restores a different kind of order. The crimes are so impossible (a woman shoots herself hours after she was already dead, a drowned man solves his lover's crossword clue, a businessman is seen by reliable witnesses on both sides of the Atlantic at the same time, a dead woman falls out of a wardrobe only moments after we see it is empty) that we need Jonathan to solve the crime. Not so the rule of law is re-imposed, but so the rules of physics are still valid. If a man can die from a gunshot wound in a sealed bunker, even though we know he was alone and too crippled with arthritis to hold the gun, let alone fire it, we need Jonathan to make sense of it all.

> Jonathan Creek doesn't look like a typical detective. There is something reassuringly normal and unthreatening about him.

> As in all good detective stories, the main character needs a sidekick or partner who is the complete opposite – here it is Maddy.

> Jonathan Creek doesn't act like a typical detective.

GLOSSARY

Crime staple: typical feature in a crime plot

Proponents: enthusiasts

Refined: improved

Labyrinthine: intricate or complicated

Morphed: changed

Tricksiness: the writer uses a made-up word to mean something tricky or confusing

Sap: a person who lacks strength and character

Baffle: confuse

Devising: coming up with

The bulk of: most of

Shrewish: bad-tempered

Upheaval: chaos or disruption

SKILLS FOCUS

✔ Understand how writers create effect through language.

✔ Recognise and understand the difference between formal and colloquial language.

✔ Understand how the writer creates tone.

LOOK CLOSER

1. Natalie Haynes has created a chatty and informal tone in her writing by using words which are not formal or standard English words. Make a list of these informal words and what you think they mean in a copy of the table below. Here is an example to start you off:

Informal word from article	Meaning
'twistiest'	Most confusing or twisty

2. Natalie Haynes often puts phrases inside brackets or separates parts of a sentence using dashes. This technique is called parenthesis. Find examples of this and explain why a reader might find these interesting. For example, in the sentence 'He's soft-hearted (those kittens do very well out of him in *The Omega Man*)', the brackets make the writer's tone sound …

3. What impression does the article create of Jonathan Creek? Copy and complete the table to organise your ideas. The first one has been done as an example.

Evidence from the text	Impression created
'magician-turned-sleuth'	This creates the impression that he isn't very experienced.
'a pleasingly unlikely detective'	It suggests …
'half genius, half sheepdog'	
'devising magic tricks for his boss'	
'the grownup version of every nerdy boy'	
'soft-hearted'	
'can be grouchy'	

4. Now write your answer to Question 3 in a paragraph.

NOW TRY THIS

1 The writer has produced a chatty and amusing account of her opinions about the television series *Jonathan Creek*. Write an entertaining article or blog about your favourite television programme or character. Think about:

- ☼ your purpose
- ☼ your intended audience
- ☼ techniques you can use to make your writing enjoyable to read.

2 You have already identified some informal words used in the article. Make a list of any informal or slang words or phrases that you and your friends use when texting or talking to each other.

FAST FINISHERS

Using your list of slang words, arrange them in alphabetical order and try to explain what they actually mean in standard English so that your parents and teachers can understand what you are talking about!

3 The words we use change depending on the situation we are in, the reason why we are speaking (purpose) and the person or people we are speaking to (audience).

(a) Imagine you are giving an account to your headteacher of a fight that has taken place in school. What would you say? Think about the language and tone you would use.

(b) With your partner, write an account of the same event as you would tell it to your friends. How would this account be different in terms of the language and tone you would use? Be prepared to read out both versions of the account to the class.

❓ PRACTICE QUESTION

Read the extract again. Choose **four** statements below which are **true**.   [4 marks]

- ☼ Copy out the ones that you think are true.
- ☼ Choose a maximum of four true statements.

A The television series *Jonathan Creek* first appeared in 1999. ☐

B Jonathan Creek is an IT technician. ☐

C *The Smiling Man* is the title of one of the episodes in the series. ☐

D Adam Klaus is Jonathan Creek's boss. ☐

E Maddy Magellan leaves to live in America. ☐

F *The Hollow Man* is a book written by John Dickson Carr. ☐

G Maddy Magellan is played by Natalie Haynes. ☐

H Edgar Allan Poe and Wilkie Collins were crime writers. ☐

12 'I'm a homicide detective in the LAPD'

From an article in the *Guardian* newspaper by Ruth Spencer
as part of the 'A day's work' series, 25 July 2013

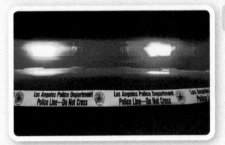

▲ An LAPD crime scene

LEARNING OBJECTIVES

- ⊙ To be able to retrieve implicit and explicit information.
- ⊙ To analyse the writer's use of language.
- ⊙ To organise ideas and information.

CONTEXT

Christopher Barling has been working with the Los Angeles police department's homicide division since 1993. He's now the homicide supervisor for the 77th division in south Los Angeles, which has historically had one of the highest murder rates in the city. In the following extract, Ruth Spencer interviews Barling about his work.

What's a typical day like for you?

First of all, there is never a typical workday for a homicide detective and since I am the homicide supervisor, I am always on call. ◄·········

> Christopher Barling always has to be available for work at any time, as he is in charge of the murder squad.

I usually start my day between 6–7am. First thing I do is meet with the members of my squad, as they get their morning cups of coffee. I then transition the conversation into getting updates on their current investigations and their investigative plans to solve their cases.

> The day often starts off with Barling checking what the members of his team will be doing that day.

Next, I determine who is going to be on call with me during the week. I then usually do a series of administrative functions: completing time sheets, signing overtime slips, reviewing search warrants, court orders, etc. But that's only the case if we didn't have a homicide overnight.

When a murder occurs, it is rarely during business hours; it is usually between 10pm and 3am. So, on those days, my watch officially starts when I arrive at the crime scene. I then assess if more detectives need to be called in and start handing out tasks to be completed. Some of the tasks can be locating and interviewing witnesses, re-canvassing the crime scene for additional witnesses or evidence, locating and downloading surveillance footage, booking evidence, searching through criminal data bases, and meeting with other law enforcement officers, who have expertise in the area where the crime occurred.

> Why do you think murders usually take place between 10 p.m. and 3 a.m.?

I oversee all of this and monitor the investigative team who is assigned the case and the teams that are assisting them.

What makes for a really good day on the job?

Barling obviously enjoys his work.

I am fortunate that every day is a good day on the job. I have the privilege of working with and supervising arguably the best detectives in the world. What makes a special day is watching the detectives put together their cases and solving them. It is satisfying to watch a team of detectives getting excited if they just got their suspect identified or have enough evidence to file a case against a murderer. If I am to use an old cliché, as homicide detectives we get to speak for the dead. It is exciting to watch a detective interviewing a suspect, and getting that suspect to make admissions or confess to a murder. It is also rewarding to hear one of the detectives get the call from the district attorney that a jury just convicted a suspect who is responsible for a murder. These days are special because we can then explain to a family that we know who is responsible for killing their loved one.

Barling is pleased that when criminals are caught and convicted, detectives can help the families have closure over what has happened to their loved ones.

How long have you been a homicide detective? What's changed over that time?

During Barling's time as a detective, his work has been helped enormously by the use of technology.

I began working as a homicide detective in 1993, and technology is the biggest change over that time. When I first started working cases, we didn't have computers. We used to handwrite all reports and then typed them on a typewriter. Now everything is done on a computer. In 1993, we just had blood typing that was used to help identity people to a crime scene. Now DNA is used, which can identify an individual using his DNA to one in a billion, quadrillion or greater. There was no social media or surveillance cameras. The technology of today has greatly helped detectives build circumstantial evidence in their cases. We now also pass information out on Twitter. Please remember, real detective work is not what you see on television shows like *Law and Order*, *CSI* and *Dexter*. We usually don't solve a case in an hour, or find scientific evidence everywhere.

Real detective work is not like the television shows, and real investigations take much longer.

What are the most difficult aspects of your job?

Over the past 10 years, 77th division has had 549 murders and there are approximately 250 open cases which are still not solved. Homicide detectives tend to be some of the most committed officers in any police agency and never want to go home without solving their case. But truth be told, we can't solve a case without the community's help and not every homicide case gets solved. However, just because it isn't solved does not mean that it is not being worked. Every year detectives solve anywhere between 60–70% of the cases, but only about 30–40% are from that calendar year. The rest of the cases, which make up the difference, are from the previous years' cases.

Detectives do not give up on investigations. Even if they do not solve the crime straightaway, it is often solved eventually.

GLOSSARY

LAPD: Los Angeles Police Department (in USA)

Homicide: murder

Supervisor: manager

Transition: move

Determine: work out

Administrative functions: paperwork tasks

Watch: shift

Assess: judge

Re-canvassing: revisiting

Surveillance footage: observation tapes

Expertise: skill

Oversee: supervise

Assigned: given

Cliché: over-used phrase

District attorney: prosecuting lawyer

Blood typing: finding out the blood group of the victim and/or criminal

Circumstantial evidence: something that suggests guilt

Approximately: roughly

SKILLS FOCUS

✔ Understand how the writer conveys feelings.

✔ Listen and respond appropriately to spoken language.

✔ Write effectively in different formats.

LOOK CLOSER

1. Find four facts that we learn about Christopher Barling in this article.

2. In 60 words or less, summarise what Christopher Barling has to do as a homicide supervisor.

3. Barling says, 'If I am to use an old cliché, as homicide detectives we get to speak for the dead.' Explain what he means by this.

4. Read the section **'How long have you been a homicide detective? What's changed over that time?'** In your own words, explain how technology has developed and changed since 1993 in helping detectives to solve crimes. Copy and complete the table to help you organise your ideas before writing your answer.

Situation in 1993	Change
'we didn't have computers'	
'We used to hand write all reports'	
'we just had blood typing to identify an individual'	
'no social media or surveillance cameras'	

NOW TRY THIS

1. This article is part of a series entitled 'A day's work'. Write an article that could be featured in this series about what you think a typical working day would be like for a teacher. You can follow the same question and answer layout if you want.

2. Do some research into the job of a police detective and present your results as a fact file. Find out information about:
   - ✪ the qualifications needed
   - ✪ training
   - ✪ salary
   - ✪ job expectations
   - ✪ working hours.

FAST FINISHERS

Using the information from your research, design an advertisement to encourage people to join the police and become a detective. Think about:
- ✪ layout
- ✪ headings
- ✪ persuasive language and techniques
- ✪ important details.

3. Christopher Barling enjoys his job as a detective. What would be your ideal job? Prepare a short presentation to deliver to your class about what your ideal job would be. Think about:
   - ✪ some details about the job
   - ✪ qualifications and training
   - ✪ why you want to do this job.

   Be ready to answer any questions the class may have.

❓ PRACTICE QUESTION

How does the article show that being a detective is a hard job? Think about what Christopher Barling has to do in his job and the language he uses to describe his work. You might want to use these sentence starters:

- ✪ The writer uses the phrase ...
- ✪ In the article, the writer gives the impression ...   [8 marks]

Los Angeles Police Department
Police Line—Do Not Cross

Los Angeles Police Department
Police Line—Do Not Cross

Los Angel
Police

From a film review by Nick Allen on www.rogerebert.com, 23 March 2018

▲ Sherlock Gnomes and Watson looking for evidence in their search for the missing gnomes

LEARNING OBJECTIVES

⊗ To be able to select information purposefully.

⊗ To analyse the writer's use of language.

⊗ To organise ideas and information.

CONTEXT

Sherlock Gnomes, the movie, was released in 2018 and is the sequel to the popular *Gnomeo and Juliet* – a humorous reworking of Shakespeare's *Romeo and Juliet*, but without the tragedy! The main characters in the film are gnomes and garden ornaments who are voiced by well-known Hollywood stars and a modern soundtrack is provided. In *Sherlock Gnomes*, the famous detective is a parody of the fictional Sherlock Holmes.

Believe it or not, 'Sherlock Gnomes' does not share the integrity of the first film. It all starts, again, with the joke of the title: this story imagines the famous detective as being too arrogant and selfish to his friend Watson and other gnomes. On top of this, this central character is brought to life with hoity-toity-ness by Johnny Depp. With little wit to its name, 'Sherlock Gnomes' becomes far more tedious than playful.

After the contained backyard chaos of 'Gnomeo and Juliet,' the franchise takes to the streets of London for a mystery that Sherlock Gnomes and his assistant Watson (Chiwetel Ejiofor) must solve. Someone has stolen all of the gnomes in London, with the trinkets vanishing randomly in the night. This includes gnomes like Lord Redbrick (Michael Caine), Lady Blueberry (Maggie Smith), Mrs Montague (Julie Walters), a fawn voiced by Ozzy Osbourne, and more. Much of the main cast returns, especially Gnomeo (James McAvoy) and Juliet (Emily Blunt), who are now imagined as a seasoned married couple that have lost touch.

The writer gives his opinion of the film and doesn't think it is as good as the previous film.

For this film, the action is set in London, where the famous detective Sherlock Gnomes lives.

The names in brackets are the famous film stars who provide voices for the animated characters.

I should say at this point that I know that this movie was not made **primarily** for someone like me. So, I am pleased to report that the most consistent piece of amusement for the crowd I saw (of **primary demographic**) was the gnome who wears sunglasses and a pink bikini. A close-up shot of his butt got the biggest laugh.

> The audience of the film is younger children and the writer gives an example of what they find funny.

Anyhow, thinking that it's his **adversary** Moriarty (now imagined as a puffy yellow pie mascot with a sharp-toothed grin and **lame meta villain jokes**, as voiced by Jamie Demetriou), the overly proud Holmes, his dutiful Watson and Gnomeo and Juliet **venture** around London, with 24 hours to find the gnomes before they are smashed. Despite these stakes, the story's sense of adventure is weak, something that I bet kids will notice (or feel in their boredom). As they go from place to place, the script **harps upon** the tension within the two pairings, especially that of how cruel Holmes is to Watson, which makes for a tediously conveyed message about not taking for granted those who support you. Nonetheless, the greatest challenge for these gnomes seems to be humans noticing their **sentience**, but would it be so bad if the gnomes were noticed? Or would that bring about a gnome **apocalypse**?

> What is the main plot of the film? Explain in your own words.

> The writer gives his opinion of the film and explains what the moral of the film is.

While the humour is certainly for kiddies and the story can't even **muster** a good twist in spite of its inspiration, the animation is more than serviceable in bringing the figures to life. There's an impressive detail to many of them, especially the shininess and the wear they individually have. It's just a case of what they do with them, which in this case is put them in a dull adventure. Opening up this franchise to small figures navigating a whole city just shows its 'Toy Story' roots more nakedly, but with forgettable characters dancing or fighting from one set-piece to the next.

> Although the plot is uninspiring, the writer praises the skill in the animation.

> The writer compares the setting to *Toy Story* but suggests that *Toy Story* is better.

'Sherlock Gnomes' is an example of how when a pun concept doesn't work, it *really* doesn't work and takes the project down with it. The new air of action doesn't lead to excitement, as the movie wants to be taken seriously for its life-or-death adventure but lacks wit. Puns are supposed to inspire cuteness in this world. But 'Sherlock Gnomes' is **bizarrely** too serious to be charming, as much as I was amused by the brief promise of gnome **genocide**.

> In the writer's opinion, the film is not a success.

GLOSSARY

Integrity: honesty

Arrogant: self-important

Hoity-toity-ness: snobbishness

Tedious: boring

Franchise: brand

Randomly: without any pattern

Seasoned: experienced

Primarily: mainly

Primary demographic: primary-aged audience

Adversary: enemy

Lame meta villain jokes: pathetic villain jokes

Venture: journey

Harps upon: keeps focused on

Sentience: wisdom

Apocalypse: end of the world

Muster: bring together

Bizarrely: strangely

Genocide: mass killing

SKILLS FOCUS

✔ Understand how writers create effect through language.

✔ Recognise and comment on the effect of writers' techniques.

✔ Understand how the writer conveys tone and attitude.

LOOK CLOSER

1 The writer uses the phrases 'arrogant and selfish to his friend Watson and other gnomes', 'hoity-toity-ness', 'how cruel Holmes is to Watson' and 'overly proud' to describe the character of Sherlock Gnomes. Explain what impression these phrases create of Sherlock Gnomes.

2 What do you think is the moral of the film?

3 The writer's attitude is mainly negative about the film. However, he does praise certain aspects of it. Read the penultimate (last but one) paragraph to find three phrases showing where the writer is impressed and explain the effect of the language used. You could use a table like this to record your findings.

Evidence from the text	Effect
'The animation is more than serviceable'	'more than' makes it sound better than average

4 Make a list of all the faults that the writer finds with the film.

FAST FINISHERS

○ Explain why the writer uses italics in the sentence '"Sherlock Gnomes" is an example of how when a pun concept doesn't work, it *really* doesn't work and takes the project down with it.'

○ What tone is the writer using in the question 'Or would that bring about a gnome apocalypse?'

NOW TRY THIS

1 Nick Allen has written a review of the film, in which he gives a very honest opinion. Write a review of a film or programme that you have recently watched. Your review can be positive or negative, or, like Nick Allen, you might find some positive and negative things to mention. Think about:

○ the plot

○ the characters and what they are like

○ the theme of the film

○ the best and worst parts

○ your recommendation.

2 Design a poster advertising the film you have reviewed. Think about a slogan or catchy heading to grab the reader's attention. What visual images would suit the film?

3 The film *Sherlock Gnomes* has a moral which is meant to teach the audience about their own lives. Write a short story which contains a moral or a lesson for the reader.

4 Imagine you have to create the voice-over for a trailer for the film *Sherlock Gnomes*. In a group of two or three, decide what you will say. Remember you want to encourage people to watch the film, so you need to make it sound fun and exciting. Be prepared to perform your trailer for the class.

❓ PRACTICE QUESTION

How does the writer use language to present his negative views of the film? Think about what the writer says and how he says it. You might want to use some of the following sentence starters:

○ The writer presents a negative view by using the phrase 'Believe it or not, "Sherlock Gnomes" does not share the integrity of the first film.' This suggests that ...

○ The line, '...', makes the reader think that ...   [8 marks]

▲ A detective conducting an interview

LEARNING OBJECTIVES

⊙ To distinguish the main ideas in a text.

⊙ To analyse the writer's use of language.

⊙ To organise ideas and information.

CONTEXT

Sophie Hannah is a crime fiction novelist. In the following extract, she writes about contacting a 'real' private detective as part of her research for a potential situation in her new novel.

Sophie looks for a respectable-looking detective agency from an internet search.

Straightaway she is disappointed by the lack of interest shown by the detective.

Sophie's husband is doubtful about how professional the detective is as he hasn't made any contact despite already being paid.

Like most people, I had never hired a private detective before. I had planned, in fact, to go my whole life without ever hiring one. Then I found myself in dire need of information that I was unable to obtain on my own, and I allowed myself to think the unthinkable: 'This is what private detectives are for, so why don't I give one a ring and see if he/she can help?' I picked the first reputable-looking, well-established firm that my Google results suggested. I should have known not to waste my money when the detective I spoke to – head of the entire agency, no less – sounded not in the least intrigued as I described to him a very weird situation. 'It's not insurance fraud and it's not infidelity,' I said by way of introduction. 'It's something much weirder than either.' Surely the only appropriate response to such a statement is, 'Ooh, tell me, tell me!' My detective sounded half asleep as he made a note of the details. He took payment in advance – £350 – and then failed to ring me back …

My husband finally managed to persuade me that my private eye was not far too busy investigating my weird conundrum to call me and give me an update; he was much more likely to be a bit rubbish, not all that bothered, and he wasn't ringing because he'd been paid already. So I swallowed my pride and phoned him, my hopes still high. I would prove my husband wrong I resolved as I made the call.

My detective sounded as if he'd forgotten my name, the names of all the other people involved in the conundrum, and, most of all, the £350 I had paid him. 'Oh, yeah,' he drawled after I had

This is a new experience for Sophie Hannah as she had never thought of using a private detective before.

jogged his memory. 'Yeah, my people spoke to a few people – and apparently there was a rumour going round that X is the case.' I could hardly believe it. 'But … but …' I stammered. 'I told *you* that there was a rumour going round that X was the case – remember?'

I almost fell over with shock. This was unbelievable. I realised that a substantial part of my problem was that, until I was unfortunate enough to encounter this useless private detective, I had met only his fictional counterparts. Fictional sleuths are all – to a man and a woman – obsessive geniuses who are happy to bend and break laws when necessary, and always get the right answer in the end, however challenging the problem, and even if it nearly kills them. They check themselves out of hospitals three seconds after emerging from surgery/a coma, against their doctors' advice. Their motto is, 'I will not rest until I uncover the truth'. By contrast, my detective's motto seemed to be, 'I *will* rest until I *don't* uncover the truth.'

Huffily, I told him that I was currently on holiday in the former holiday home of the great Agatha Christie – creator of Hercule Poirot and Miss Marple. I hoped that the mention of these superior detectives would fire him up, spur him on to do better. It didn't. Finally, I had no choice but to boss him around. I told him the names of three people who would definitely know the truth. All he had to do, I suggested, was adopt a fake name, infiltrate their lives in some way. At this point, I think I said, 'Do I *really* have to go on? I mean … surely you've watched some of the same movies and read some of the same books I have?' He declared himself reluctant to use aliases and/or disguises, and unwilling to commute. He told me how much the extra work I was urging upon him would cost. That was when I began to despair. What kind of detective refuses to pretend to be someone else in order to gain the trust of a key witness? I got so angry, I eventually produced a massively hackneyed phrase: 'I don't care how you get the answer. Just think of something you *are* willing to do, and *get the answer.*'

I waited for him to ring me back. He didn't. Eventually I rang him and, once again, reminded him of my name, situation and bank account depleted to the tune of £350. 'Oh, right, yes,' my detective said in a vague tone of voice … For a brief, strange moment, I considered hiring a new, better private detective to investigate whether the first private detective was lying to me.

GLOSSARY

Dire: serious

Reputable: well respected

Intrigued: fascinated

Infidelity: being unfaithful in a marriage

In advance: before doing the job

Conundrum: problem or puzzle

Resolved: determined

Drawled: spoke slowly and lazily

Counterparts: equivalent

To a man and woman: every single one

Motto: saying

Huffily: with annoyance

Infiltrate: gain access to

Aliases: false names

Hackneyed: over-used

SKILLS FOCUS

✔ Understand how writers create effect through language.

✔ Understand how writers use sentence length to create effect.

✔ Understand how the writer creates tone.

LOOK CLOSER

1 Sophie Hannah doesn't think that the detective is good at his job. How does she use language to suggest that he is not a good detective? Use the examples below as a starting point, but also find evidence of your own from the article. Copy and complete the table.

Evidence from the text	Effect of language
'not in the least intrigued'	This creates the impression that …
'sounded half asleep'	
'payment in advance'	
'failed to ring me back'	
'he drawled'	

2 In paragraph 4, the writer uses sentences of different lengths. Find two examples of short sentences and explain what effect they create.

3 What impression does the article give of the relationship between Sophie Hannah and her husband? Think about what the husband says and does and how Sophie reacts.

4 In the penultimate (last but one) paragraph, the writer uses different types of punctuation including rhetorical questions and ellipsis. Find examples of these and explain what effect they create.

NOW TRY THIS

1 The writer clearly feels let down by the detective and disappointed by his attitude. Write about a time when you felt let down by someone.

2 Imagine you are Sophie. Write an online review of the detective agency. You might want to think about these headings:

- customer satisfaction
- reliability
- communication
- value for money
- recommendation.

FAST FINISHERS

Write the online advertisement for the detective agency that Sophie would have seen. Think about:

- a catchy slogan or heading
- what services are being advertised
- persuasive words and phrases to grab the reader's attention
- anything else you think is important.

3 Sophie was unhappy with the service she received from the detective agency. Imagine you have received poor service in a restaurant or a shop and you decide to complain. With a partner, produce a script of the confrontation. Be prepared to act out the scene in front of the class.

❓ PRACTICE QUESTION

Read the article again. What impression do we have of Sophie Hannah? Remember to track from the beginning to the end of the article and use evidence to prove your points. Think about:

- what Sophie thinks and does at the start of the article
- how and why Sophie's attitude to the detective changes
- what Sophie thinks and does at the end of the article.   [8 marks]

15 The Timeless Secret of Nancy Drew

Adapted from an article by Amanda Festa on www.literarytraveler.com, 24 July 2013

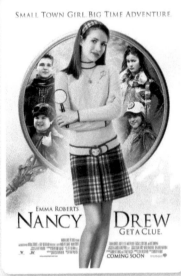

SMALL TOWN GIRL. BIG TIME ADVENTURE.

EMMA ROBERTS

NANCY DREW
GET A CLUE.

COMING SOON

▲ Nancy Drew as she
appears in a 2007 film

LEARNING OBJECTIVES

- To select evidence purposefully.
- To analyse the writer's use of language.
- To organise ideas and information.

CONTEXT

In this article, Amanda Festa writes about her love of reading and how the fictional teenage detective Nancy Drew inspired her. The series of *Nancy Drew Mysteries* was written by Carolyn Keene and has been popular with young teenagers from the 1930s to the present day.

> Amanda Festa believes that reading Nancy Drew books has made her the person she is now.

> When she was young, Amanda used to imagine she was having the adventures with the character.

Discovering Nancy Drew was one of those moments in life that defined me – which I understand sounds a little drastic. It's only a book series, right? When you're young and your curiosity is piqued, the smallest things can impact your life in the biggest ways. Some kids had sports; I had books – an awkward, bespectacled little girl who lived vicariously through the bold strawberry-blonde detective as she set out on exciting adventures.

My mom shared Nancy with me, a remnant of her own childhood. She helped me collect all fifty-six of the shiny yellow-spine 'flashlight editions,' which sat proudly on a bookshelf above my desk. She would tell me with dismay of how her mom had discarded her own collection, and how she wished she'd still had them to pass along to me.

> Amanda and her mother were able to share an interest in Nancy Drew and bond over their love of the books.

> What do you think Amanda means by saying that 'Nancy was both inspiration and escape'?

Nancy was both inspiration and escape. As clichéd as it sounds, I read my sturdy 'flashlight editions' by flashlight curled up on a canopy bed under a dusty-rose duvet in the hopes that I wouldn't wake my sister, who was never a big reader and wouldn't understand my urgency to finish the next chapter – or six. Every little girl has a role model, and Nancy was mine. She was strong and independent, decisive and brave. She protected her friends, maintained her independence, and was always quick to pack a suitcase and be off on a spontaneous adventure. I may not have a little blue roadster (or the ability to drive it), but I have great friends, an independent spirit, and a wanderlust that has yet to be quenched. Thanks, Nancy.

Amanda admires all the qualities that the fictional teenage detective had and feels she has developed similar qualities herself in her adult life.

First published in 1930, Nancy Drew was created to expand on the publishing group's previous success with children's mystery stories such as *The Hardy Boys* as to include books targeted to the female demographic. In existence for over 80 years, Nancy Drew remains the courageous amateur detective that she has always been, but aside from her penchant for a good mystery, she is barely recognizable in 2013 from her original manifestation. Trading telegram for text message, and shift dresses for tank tops – Nancy has changed with the times. Yet, despite superficial wardrobe updates and technological advances, she remains timeless.

Times have changed since Nancy Drew's first adventure but the character has adapted and changed with the times to be relevant to modern audiences.

And I am not alone. Nancy Drew is an icon for a reason – because children have found themselves in her, found strength in her, and escaped with her. I know countless individuals, traveling very different paths in life, who all cite Nancy as a central figure – including, of course, Nancy Drew Sleuths president, Jennifer Fisher.

Nancy Drew Sleuths began as an internet discussion group in 2000, quickly expanding into a fan club that features gatherings, conventions and a comprehensive website that is a go-to wealth of Nancy knowledge. Like myself and countless others, Fisher grew up captivated by the girl detective. 'One of my first memories,' she admits, 'is reading the books in my school library and being so fascinated by the stories to the point of sitting near them during library lessons so I could peek in them.'

The character of Nancy Drew has become such a role model that a fan club has been established called 'Nancy Drew Sleuths' (detectives) in honour of the character.

In addition to her research, writing and collecting, Fisher plans the annual Nancy Drew Sleuths conventions. The first one took place in Toledo, Ohio in 2001, although, according to Fisher, 'it wasn't considered a convention at the time, just a gathering of a small group of around 12 fans, but it was so much fun that we started planning them for each year after that.'

Fan conventions are held every year and are continuing to grow in popularity.

The conventions take place in a new location each year, picked based on the setting of a Nancy Drew mystery, and the theme of the convention involves exploring the real-life locations featured in that particular book. Fisher admits, 'We do have quite a few regulars – generally about 20 to 30 come just about every year. Though that number is growing as the years go by! I think it's like a family reunion in some ways seeing each other again each year, we really have a lot of fun!' Newbies fit right in and quickly become part of the Sleuth family through five days of activities, sightseeing, and conversation – bonding over their own unique ties to the popular girl sleuth.

Everyone is welcome at the conventions and there are many activities to enjoy and opportunities to bond with new members.

GLOSSARY

Defined: established who I was
Piqued: excited or stirred
Impact: have an effect on
Bespectacled: wearing glasses
Vicariously: indirectly
Remnant: left over
Discarded: thrown away
Clichéd: unoriginal
Flashlight: torch
Decisive: determined
Spontaneous: unplanned or spur of the moment
Roadster: small car

Wanderlust: a desire to travel
Quenched: put out or extinguished
Demographic: audience
Penchant: liking for
Manifestation: appearance
Shift dress: a simple, sleeveless dress, popular in the 1960s
Tank top: a sleeveless sports top or vest top
Icon: idol
Cite: praise
Comprehensive: extensive

SKILLS FOCUS

✔ Understand how writers create effects through language.
✔ Develop confidence in delivering an individual presentation.
✔ Develop skills for descriptive writing.

LOOK CLOSER

1. Read paragraphs 1 and 2 again. What impression do you have of the writer as a young girl? Fill in a copy of the table to organise your ideas.

Evidence from the text	Impression
'I had books'	This implies …
'awkward'	The adjective creates the impression …
'bespectacled little girl'	
'lived vicariously through the bold strawberry-blonde detective'	
'collected all 56 of the shiny yellow-spine "flashlight editions"'	
'sat proudly'	

2. Read paragraph 3 again. In your own words, summarise the qualities that make Nancy Drew such an attractive and interesting character.

3. Amanda Festa writes, 'Nancy Drew is an icon for a reason – because children have found themselves in her, found strength in her, and escaped with her.' Explain what she means by this.

4. List four facts about the Nancy Drew Sleuths and the conventions they hold.

NOW TRY THIS

1 Amanda Festa considered Nancy Drew to be a role model who inspired her. Write an account of a person who is an inspirational role model for you.

- You might want to write about a member of your family, a teacher, a sports person or anyone else of your choice.
- Write about the qualities that you admire in this person.
- Write about what this person does to inspire you.
- Use interesting adjectives and verbs to make your account vivid.

2 Amanda Festa and her mother loved reading about the adventures of Nancy Drew. Think about a book or series of books that you have really enjoyed reading. Write a review of the book you have chosen in order to persuade your classmates to read it also. Remember to include:

- what the book is about (without giving away the ending!)
- why you enjoyed it
- description of the main character(s)
- why you would recommend it
- recommended age group.

FAST FINISHERS

- Write the 'blurb' that you think should appear on the back of the book to attract the reader and persuade him or her to choose to read it.
- Design an eye-catching front cover for the book you are recommending.

3 The Nancy Drew books are clearly very special possessions for Amanda and her mother. What possessions do you have that hold special meanings or are connected with special memories for you? Prepare a presentation that you will deliver to the class entitled 'My Treasured Possessions'. What will you say and how will you deliver your presentation? Think about:

- how you will grab your audience's attention at the start
- how you will vary the openings of your sentences to keep their attention
- the interesting and varied vocabulary you will use.

❓ PRACTICE QUESTION

How does the writer make the article interesting for the reader?
Think about:

- what the article is about
- the relationship between the writer and her mother
- the influence *Nancy Drew* has had on the writer
- the Nancy Drew Sleuths and their conventions
- the ending of the text. [8 marks]

16 Police Now

From an advertisement for police recruitment

▲ Police on duty

CONTEXT

The advertisement below is taken from the Police Now campaign to attract new recruits into the police force to become detectives.

The logo and catchphrase for the organisation.

POLICE:NOW
INFLUENCE FOR GENERATIONS

A heading to attract attention.

HAVE A POSITIVE IMPACT ON SOCIETY, BECOME A DETECTIVE

WHY CHOOSE A CAREER AS A DETECTIVE?

Do you notice? Are you inquisitive? A problem solver? Someone who can communicate with anyone? Can you gain the trust of those around you?

Do you approach ongoing challenges with focus and determination? Do you have the resilience to see it through to conclusion?

Why does the advert use so many questions directed to the reader?

Choosing to be a detective is a serious career choice. Detectives are focused, work well under pressure and respond quickly to new information with a determined, positive attitude.

A career as a detective offers a competitive starting salary and benefits package compared to other graduate career choices, alongside long-term career development. You also get a unique chance to have an immediate and positive impact on the most vulnerable people in society.

The advert uses many adjectives to influence the reader.

Join one of our partner police forces as a trainee detective through Police Now's National Detective Programme.

WHAT DO DETECTIVES DO?

Are you emotionally aware? Do you see things from other points of view? Can you quickly form meaningful relationships across diverse groups of people?

Subheadings are used to sum up what the paragraph(s) will be about.

You're a methodical and analytical problem solver. You have the ability to foresee risks and don't jump to conclusions, but gather all the information before making a call.

Does this sound like you? If so, you have the potential to become a detective.

CRIME IS CHANGING, AND SO ARE WE

The Police Now National Detective Programme has been designed to equip you with the core policing skills required in modern investigative work, with a strong emphasis on digital training, allowing you to contribute to the outstanding work already being done by existing detectives up and down the country. ◄········

> A description of some of the training is given.

Successful candidates will be resilient, focusing on working towards defined goals, rarely losing focus. You'll be tenacious, the type of person who makes a choice and sticks with it. By demonstrating a positive can-do attitude, you will view obstacles differently to everyone else – there to be tackled head-on rather than used as an excuse to give up. ◄········

> The qualities needed for this type of work are described.

We're looking for talented and driven individuals who notice what others would miss. As a detective you will quickly become an instrumental member of the police force, solving crimes and working towards making our communities safer places to live, for generations to come. Join us.

- Learn to lead with conviction, right from the start.
- Training led by police detectives with years of experience solving crimes across the UK.
- Build your resilience and communication skills whilst developing your innate curiosity.
- Become a great investigative detective, keeping the public safe for generations to come. ◄········

> Bullet points are listed to show the benefits that can be gained by becoming a detective.

Here we share the stories of a graduate who started her journey with Police Now to give you an insight into life as a detective in the forces.

DC GABALDI

DC Gabaldi had never met a police officer before she applied to join the police. Helping people has always been central to why she loves working in the police. As a police constable she was often first on the scene, however her new career as a detective means her role has evolved, and she now has the ongoing responsibility to manage cases and to think strategically in order to solve a crime.

> The real life account of a detective's career is included to interest the reader.

As a detective constable she has adjusted to the challenging nature of the areas of work she has gained experience in so far. ◄········

She is driven by her own mission of working to protect the victims of crime that she meets every single day from future harm. She often takes time to reflect on how her short career to date as a detective has already exposed her to a wide range of backgrounds and experiences, all very different to her Italian roots. What she is learning about humans and how they behave is also teaching her some important lessons about the fabric of society. ◄········

> As a detective, you will learn about people and how they behave as well as skills needed for solving crimes.

GLOSSARY

Impact: effect

Inquisitive: curious or nosey

Ongoing: continuing

Resilience: strength of character

Focused: single-minded

Competitive: as good as

Graduate: a person who has been to university and gained a degree

Unique: one of a kind

Vulnerable: weak

Diverse: varied

Methodical: well organised

Analytical: logical

Foresee: predict

Potential: ability

Core: essential

Defined: set out

Tenacious: persistent and determined

Instrumental: an influence

Evolved: changed

Strategically: in a well thought-out way

Adjusted: changed

Mission: purpose

Fabric of society: make-up of society

SKILLS FOCUS

✔ Understand how the writer uses language and techniques to persuade.

✔ Listen and respond appropriately to spoken language.

✔ Write effectively in different formats.

LOOK CLOSER

1. Now read the paragraph 'Why Choose a Career as a Detective?' very carefully again. The advertisement uses some important language features. Copy and complete the table below, finding at least one example of each language feature and the effect that it has on the reader.

Language feature	Examples	Effect on the reader
Questions		
Second person direct address (you)		
Adjectives	'Inquisitive', 'focused'	
Commands or imperatives		

2 Read the section 'What Do Detectives Do?' again. In your own words, explain what qualities you would need in order to be a successful detective.

3 What impression of the police force does the advertisement give the reader? Copy and complete the table below and explain the effect that the word/phrase has on the reader.

Evidence from the text	Impression created
'Police Now'	The adverb 'now' suggests that …
'influence for generations'	
'Crime is changing, and so are we'	
'a detective is a serious career choice'	
'competitive starting salary'	

NOW TRY THIS

1 This advert is designed to persuade people to apply to join the police force and become detectives. Write a persuasive advertisement to persuade people to apply to become teachers. Think about:
   - ✪ using persuasive language and techniques
   - ✪ an appropriate layout with headings and sub-headings
   - ✪ a logo or design to use in the advert.

2 One of the qualities needed to be a detective is having the resilience to see something through to the end. Write an account of a time when you had to be resilient and overcome challenges.

FAST FINISHERS
Design a brand new logo and motto to represent the police force.

3 This advertisement has many persuasive words and techniques to encourage people to join the police force. Prepare a persuasive speech in which you try to encourage your classmates to take up your favourite sport or hobby. Deliver the speech to your classmates and be prepared to answer questions.

❓ PRACTICE QUESTION

How does the advertisement try to persuade you to become a detective? Remember to think about **what** the advertisement says and **the words** it uses to persuade you.

For example, the advertisement tries to persuade you to become a detective by explaining what the job actually involves. Words like 'challenges', 'focus' and 'determination' sound exciting and are persuasive because you want to imagine yourself doing exciting things. [8 marks]

Section 3: Poetry

17 The Bloodhound
by Laura Leiser

▲ A bloodhound ready to track a scent

LEARNING OBJECTIVES

- ✪ To distinguish main ideas and select relevant points from the texts.
- ✪ To show awareness of how language choices affect meaning.
- ✪ To examine mood and atmosphere.

CONTEXT

The following poem was written in 2019 by Laura Leiser, who is an American poet living in California. Bloodhounds are large dogs, originally bred for hunting deer and wild boar, but, since the Middle Ages, they have been bred for tracking people as they can pick up the scent of a human and follow it over great distances. These dogs have been used by police and law enforcement agencies to search for missing people and criminals alike.

In the poem, the events are narrated in first person narrative from the point of view of the bloodhound.

Dawn breaks over the horizon in a thin, frail line
my large snout presses downward upon the
ragged earth beneath, for I am on the hunt
absorbed in my task, scanning and searching
for that elusive scent that is in my wake.

Like a great detective, I will leave no stone unturned
I am proud of my prodigious nose, finely tuned
precise as a compass, I can detect the rarest
of scents, however miniscule, and will probe
follow that unique smell, to find what is lost …
it is the zenith of my existence.

What, ho! Now, the scent!
My body trembles with the thrill of discovery!
Onward, I go, with eager anticipation
I will not stop until I reach my destination.

Alas, my determination pays off
my master sees the end in sight …
I do not understand his sudden sadness
how he draws back at the scene set before him.

The poem is written in first person narrative, from the point of view of the bloodhound.

The bloodhound is highly skilled and well trained to do his job.

The poet uses ellipsis here to create suspense and anticipation for the reader.

The poet uses exclamations here to make the tone of the poem one of excitement and tension.

There is another change in tone here as the reader is intrigued by the reaction of the bloodhound's master.

As I nuzzle close to my master
his salty tears drench my face
my doleful eyes seem to comfort him
as we huddle together underneath the dry, hot sun.

What mood is created at the end of the poem by phrases such as 'his salty tears', 'my doleful eyes seem to comfort him' and 'we huddle together'?

GLOSSARY

Frail: weak

Snout: nose

Absorbed in: completely occupied by

Elusive: difficult to find

Wake: path

Leave no stone unturned: search everywhere

Prodigious: enormous

Precise: accurate

Miniscule: tiny

Probe: explore

Zenith: high point

Nuzzle: snuggle

Doleful: sad

SKILLS FOCUS

✔ Understand the meaning of the poem.

✔ Analyse the writer's use of language.

✔ Analyse mood and atmosphere.

LOOK CLOSER

1 Read the poem again. Summarise what happens in each stanza of the poem. Fill in a copy of the table below with your summary.

Stanza	What happens
1	The bloodhound starts tracking a scent.
2	We learn that the bloodhound …
3	
4	
5	

2 In stanza 2, the bloodhound is presented as a proud creature. Explain how the poet creates this impression by completing a copy of the table.

Evidence	Impression created
'like a great detective'	
'my prodigious nose, finely tuned'	
'I can detect the rarest of scents'	
'follow that unique smell'	

3 Explain why the poet has used an ellipsis at the end of these lines in stanza 4:
'Alas, my determination pays off
my master sees the end in sight …'

4 Read the final stanza again. How does the poet suggest that there is a close relationship between the bloodhound and his master?

NOW TRY THIS

1 Write a lively account of a time when you were helped by or relied on an animal or pet. The account can be factual or fictional.

2 Imagine you are the master of the bloodhound. Write a diary entry describing the events of the day and what you discover. Think about:

- what or who you are looking for
- your relationship with the bloodhound
- what you discover
- your thoughts and feelings
- how the bloodhound behaves.

FAST FINISHERS

Research some animals who have become well known for helping humans. The animals and events can be factual or fictional (from stories or films). Present your information as a fact file or poster.

3 With a partner, decide which five of the following adjectives best describe the bloodhound in the poem. Be prepared to defend your decisions to the class by explaining your choices with reference to the poem.

arrogant	sympathetic
reliable	lonely
experienced	selfish
skilful	loyal
easily distracted	caring
trustworthy	smug

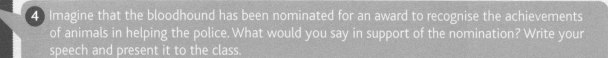

4 Imagine that the bloodhound has been nominated for an award to recognise the achievements of animals in helping the police. What would you say in support of the nomination? Write your speech and present it to the class.

❓ PRACTICE QUESTION

Read the poem again. How has the poet structured the poem to interest the reader? Write three paragraphs. Here are some sentence starters to help you.

⭐ **Paragraph 1**

At the start of the poem, there is a ＿＿＿＿＿＿＿ mood.

For example, the poet writes …

This makes the poem interesting because …

⭐ **Paragraph 2**

In the third stanza of the poem, the mood changes and becomes …

For example, the poet writes …

This intrigues the reader because …

⭐ **Paragraph 3**

Finally, at the end of the poem, the mood is …

For example, the poet …

I think the mood has changed from the beginning because … [8 marks]

18 What Has Happened to Lulu?

by Charles Causley

▲ The ragdoll left by Lulu

LEARNING OBJECTIVES

- To recognise implicit and explicit ideas in a text.
- To understand how the poet uses structure.
- To show awareness of how language choices affect meaning.

CONTEXT

Charles Causley was an English poet who was born in 1917 and died in 2003. This poem is written in the form of a ballad, which tells a story of an event in four-line stanzas with a clear rhyme scheme. Causley was well known for writing simple, direct poems.

The poem is told from the point of view of Lulu's sister, who is a young child.

What has happened to Lulu, mother?
What has happened to Lu?
There's nothing in her bed but an old rag-doll
And by its side a shoe.

Why is her window wide, mother,
The curtain flapping free,
And only a circle on the dusty shelf
Where her money-box used to be?

The young sister doesn't understand what has happened and is asking her mother questions.

The mother is not giving any answers but is clearly upset because of what has happened.

Why do you turn your head, mother,
And why do tear drops fall?
And why do you crumple that note on the fire
And say it is nothing at all?

I woke to voices late last night,
I heard an engine roar.
Why do you tell me the things I heard
Were a dream and nothing more?

Why do you think the mother lies to the younger sister?

I heard somebody cry, mother,
In anger or in pain,
But now I ask you why, mother,
You say it was a gust of rain.

Who was crying 'in anger or in pain'?

The narrator uses the affectionate abbreviation 'Lu' when talking about her sister.

Why do you wander about as though
You don't know what to do?
What has happened to Lulu, mother?
What has happened to Lu?

74

GLOSSARY

Rag-doll: a soft doll made from cloth

SKILLS FOCUS

✔ Understand and summarise the poem.
✔ Produce a piece of imaginative writing.
✔ Listen and respond appropriately to others.

▲ Lulu's shoe

LOOK CLOSER

1 Read the poem again. Make a copy of the table below and draw a storyboard summarising what happens in the poem, using the captions for each stanza to help you.

1	2	3
What has happened to Lulu, mother?	The curtain flapping free,	And why do you crumple that note on the fire …?
4	5	6
I heard an engine roar.	I heard somebody cry, mother,	What has happened to Lu?

2 Read stanza 3 again. The mother turns her head away from the narrator and she crumples the note in the fire. Explain why she behaves like this.

3 How do you think the narrator is feeling about what has happened? Choose six adjectives from the following list and explain your choices with reference to the poem.

pleased	sad
confused	jealous
angry	inquisitive
bewildered	upset
dejected	hurt
ignored	protected

4 What do you think has happened to Lulu? What clues are there in the poem to make you reach this conclusion?

NOW TRY THIS

1 Write the letter that Lulu has left for her family. Think about:
- ✪ what might have happened to make her want to leave
- ✪ how she is feeling
- ✪ how she feels about the members of her family
- ✪ the language she uses.

2 You are the detective who has been called to investigate the mysterious disappearance of Lulu. What questions would you ask the mother and sister? Remember to ask as many 'open' questions as you can because you need to find out as much information as possible.

3 In a group of three, turn the events of the poem into a piece of drama. Aim to make up two scenes. The first scene could be an argument or confrontation that Lulu has with her mother that leads to her leaving; the second scene could be the discovery of and reaction to her disappearance the next morning.

Set the scenes out as a play script and remember to indicate stage directions and the tone of voice being used.

Be prepared to act the scenes out in front of your class.

FAST FINISHERS

Imagine that Lulu realises that her family will be worried about her so she decides to contact her younger sister to let her know that she is safe. What would Lulu say and what would her sister want to know? Improvise the scene with a partner and then act it out for your class.

❓ PRACTICE QUESTION

Read the extract again. Choose **four** statements below which
are **true**. [4 marks]

⊙ Copy out the ones that you think are true.

⊙ Choose a maximum of four true statements.

A Lulu left the house through the front door. ☐

B The mother is very upset. ☐

C Lulu took her rag-doll with her. ☐

D The younger sister knows where Lulu has gone. ☐

E The mother threw the note from Lulu on the fire. ☐

F Lulu was collected from the house by someone in a car. ☐

G Lulu didn't take any of her money with her. ☐

H The younger sister heard voices the night Lulu left. ☐

19 Macavity the Mystery Cat
by T S Eliot

▲ Macavity the Mystery Cat

LEARNING OBJECTIVES

⊗ To distinguish main ideas and select relevant points from the text.

⊗ To explore the writer's presentation of character.

⊗ To analyse the writer's use of language and techniques in a poem.

CONTEXT

Macavity the Mystery Cat is a fictional character in T S Eliot's poetry book *Old Possum's Book of Practical Cats*. He also appears in the Andrew Lloyd Webber musical *Cats*, which is based on Eliot's book. Macavity is a top criminal who always outwits the police. T S Eliot (1888–1965) was a fan of the Sherlock Holmes mysteries and Macavity is thought to be based on the character of Professor Moriarty, Holmes' great enemy.

Macavity's a Mystery Cat: he's called the Hidden Paw –
For he's the master criminal who can defy the Law.
He's the bafflement of Scotland Yard, the Flying Squad's despair:
For when they reach the scene of crime – Macavity's not there!

> Macavity has been given the nickname 'Hidden Paw' because the detectives are never able to catch him.

Macavity, Macavity, there's no one like Macavity,
He's broken every human law, he breaks the law of gravity.
His powers of levitation would make a fakir stare,
And when you reach the scene of crime – Macavity's not there!
You may seek him in the basement, you may look up in the air –
But I tell you once and once again, Macavity's not there!

> **Why is the phrase 'Macavity's not there!' repeated in this stanza? Why has the poet used an exclamation mark at the end?**

Macavity's a ginger cat, he's very tall and thin;
You would know him if you saw him, for his eyes are sunken in.
His brow is deeply lined with thought, his head is highly domed;
His coat is dusty from neglect, his whiskers are uncombed.
He sways his head from side to side, with movements like a snake;
And when you think he's half asleep, he's always wide awake.

> Macavity is a cunning character who might appear to be innocent and harmless but he is always alert and planning his next move.

Macavity, Macavity, there's no one like Macavity,
For he's a fiend in feline shape, a monster of depravity.
You may meet him in a by-street, you may see him in the square –
But when a crime's discovered, then Macavity's not there!

> Macavity parades around during the day but when a crime has been committed, Macavity can never be found.

Since he is a cat, some of Macavity's crimes are ones we can imagine a cat doing. Others are more unusual! What crimes is Macavity associated with in this stanza?

When detectives are looking for Macavity, he is a long way from where the crime occurred and appears to be harmless and innocent.

Macavity is also thought to have committed crimes that are much more serious.

Why is the phrase, 'MACAVITY WASN'T THERE!' written in capital letters?

Macavity is described as the 'Napoleon of Crime'. This is the same phrase that Conan Doyle used to describe Professor Moriarty in the Sherlock Holmes stories.

He's outwardly respectable. (They say he cheats at cards.)
And his footprints are not found in any file of Scotland Yard's
And when the larder's looted, or the jewel-case is rifled,
Or when the milk is missing, or another Peke's been stifled,
Or the greenhouse glass is broken, and the trellis past repair –
Ay, there's the wonder of the thing! Macavity's not there!

And when the Foreign Office find a Treaty's gone astray,
Or the Admiralty lose some plans and drawings by the way,
There may be a scrap of paper in the hall or on the stair –
But it's useless to investigate – Macavity's not there!
And when the loss has been disclosed, the Secret Service say:
'It must have been Macavity!' – but he's a mile away.
You'll be sure to find him resting, or a-licking of his thumbs,
Or engaged in doing complicated long division sums.

Macavity, Macavity, there's no one like Macavity,
There never was a Cat of such deceitfulness and suavity.
He always has an alibi, and one or two to spare:
At whatever time the deed took place – MACAVITY WASN'T THERE!
And they say that all the Cats whose wicked deeds are widely known,
(I might mention Mungojerrie, I might mention Griddlebone)
Are nothing more than agents for the Cat who all the time
Just controls their operations: the Napoleon of Crime.

GLOSSARY

Defy: refuse to obey
Bafflement: embarrassment
Scotland Yard: Police Headquarters
Flying Squad: Special Crime Force
The law of gravity: the forces of nature
Levitation: floating into the air
Fakir: mystical man
Domed: arched
Fiend: devil
Feline: cat
Depravity: wickedness
Outwardly respectable: appearing to be honest
Larder's looted: food cupboard is raided
Rifled: burgled
Peke's been stifled: a small Pekinese dog has been smothered
Trellis: pretty garden fencing
Foreign Office: a government department looking after British issues abroad

Treaty's gone astray: an agreement has gone missing

Admiralty: a government department for defence

Disclosed: made known

Secret Service: a government department of spies

Engaged in: busy doing

Suavity: charm and sophistication

Alibi: a cover for

Mungojerrie, Griddlebone: fictional cat thieves

Napoleon of Crime: criminal mastermind

SKILLS FOCUS

✔ Summarise the meaning of the poem.

✔ Understand and analyse the writer's use of language.

✔ Produce a piece of writing with an appropriate format and tone.

LOOK CLOSER

1 Read the poem again. Now draw a storyboard like the one on p 75, summarising what happens, with one scene for each stanza. Think of a suitable caption to describe what is happening in each stanza.

2 The poem contains some interesting language features. Fill in a copy of the table below, analysing the language that Eliot uses. The first row has been done for you.

Evidence	Language feature	Effect
'with movements like a snake'	simile	This suggests that Macavity can move stealthily and quietly. It also suggests that he is sly and cunning like a snake.
'a monster of depravity'	Metaphor	
'a fiend in feline shape'		
'(They say he cheats at cards.)'		
'Or when the milk is missing, or another Peke's been stifled, or the greenhouse glass is broken'		

3 There are two sides to Macavity's character and he is not always what he seems. Explain what the following quotes suggest about Macavity's character:

(a) 'There never was a Cat of such deceitfulness and suavity.'

(b) 'He's outwardly respectable. (They say he cheats at cards.)'

4 If you had to make up an alternative title for the poem, what would you choose and why?

NOW TRY THIS

1 Write a front-page newspaper article reporting some of the crimes that Macavity has committed. Think about:

- layout
- choice of headline
- picture and caption
- the 5Ws: who, where, what, when, why
- interviews with bystanders and detectives.

2 Based on the description of Macavity in the poem, write the fact file that detectives at Scotland Yard might have compiled about him. You can use the following headings to start, and add any of your own.

- Height
- Weight
- Breed
- Colour
- Age
- Distinguishing features or special markings
- Characteristics
- Skills

FAST FINISHERS

Using the information in your fact file, produce a 'WANTED' poster for the capture of Macavity that Scotland Yard could use.

3 Imagine that Macavity has finally been caught and arrested. You are the detective in charge of carrying out the interview with this master criminal. With your partner, role play the interview and be prepared to act it out for the class.

4 Macavity's case has been brought to trial in court. You are the lawyer defending him. Write the speech you would make to defend his actions and prove his innocence.

Be prepared to deliver your speech in class.

❓ PRACTICE QUESTION

Read the poem again. How has Eliot used language to present the character of Macavity? Here are some sentence starters to help you:

- Firstly, Eliot uses ...
- For example, he writes ...
- This makes Macavity seem clever because ...
- Eliot uses the phrase 'There's no one like Macavity' to suggest ...
- The simile 'movement like a snake' ... presents Macavity as being ...
- I have the impression that Macavity is ... from the words ...

[8 marks]

20 Inspector Tweede

by Robert L Hinshaw

▲ Inspector Tweede in his tweed suit

LEARNING OBJECTIVES

- ✪ To distinguish main ideas and select relevant points from a text.
- ✪ To make inferences about a character.
- ✪ To explore writers' techniques.

CONTEXT

Robert L Hinshaw is a modern American poet. His poem 'Inspector Tweede' won first prize in a competition to write a piece on the theme of mystery. It is written in five, regular, four-line stanzas. It has a clear rhyme scheme, where the first two lines and last two lines of the stanza rhyme, giving it a humorous tone.

There was no finer detective than Inspector Thaddeus Tweede of Scotland Yard!
He was most astute in solving crimes and could quickly detect a fake canard!
He joined the force as a 'bobby' working himself to the peak of his profession.
You daren't pull the wool over his eyes when he was seeking a confession!

Ah! He could have been cast in a movie since he was a detective's prototype,
In his tweed suit, tweed cape, tweed deerstalker's cap and ever-present pipe!
When investigating crime scenes he'd mull the facts with his chin in his hand,
Puffing his pipe making copious notes should he be called to the witness stand!

The highlight of his career was solving the case of Prime Minister Percival Hoar,
Who was found by his maid one dark and stormy night sprawled upon the floor!
There was no evidence of forceful entry or anyone breaking through the door,
Nor was there any sign of a struggle, bullet holes or oozing, bloody gore!

Inspector Thaddeus Tweede is a hardworking detective who has worked his way up the career ladder from starting as an ordinary 'bobby' to becoming an inspector.

Inspector Tweede looks like an old fashioned detective because he has some of the same clothes and accessories associated with the great fictional detective, Sherlock Holmes.

Percival Hoar is a fictional Prime Minister and Inspector Tweede was called to investigate his mysterious death.

Who could have done this **dastardly** deed that brought the minister to his **doom**?
He took prints, photos and noted a strange **odor** as he moved about the room.
Thaddeus called on all his experience and training to solve this mysterious case,
Muttering to himself and doing a lot of 'hmming' as to and fro he did pace!

Eureka! He noted a bulge in the prime minister's jacket he hadn't noticed before!
Gingerly lifting a bottle from the pocket he **deduced** he needn't search anymore.
It wasn't a gun, the butler, **jilted lover**, political enemy or an envious friend
That did the terrible deed – 'twas demon rum that brought the minister to his end!

> What type of question is being asked in this line?

> The poet uses exclamations here to show that Inspector Tweede has made a sudden discovery.

> The cause of Percival Hoar's death is revealed – he died from drinking too much.

GLOSSARY

Scotland Yard: Police headquarters

Astute: intelligent

Canard: lie

'Bobby': policeman

Prototype: original version

Tweed: a rough woollen fabric

Cape: a sleeveless cloak

Deerstalker's cap: a hat often worn for hunting

Mull: think about

Copious: very many

Dastardly: wicked

Doom: terrible fate

Odor: smell

Eureka!: a cry of satisfaction when something is discovered

Gingerly: carefully

Deduced: worked out

Jilted lover: rejected girlfriend

SKILLS FOCUS

✔ Understand implicit and explicit meanings.

✔ Appreciate and analyse the writer's use of language.

✔ Produce a lively piece of writing.

LOOK CLOSER

1 In the first stanza, we learn that Inspector Tweede is good at his job. Fill in a copy of this table to explain the effect of each of the words and phrases.

Evidence	Effect
'no finer detective'	
'astute'	
'quickly detect'	
'working himself to the peak of his profession'	This implies that he is determined to succeed and is ambitious for promotion.
'You daren't pull the wool over his eyes'	

2 The poet uses some interesting verbs, adjectives and adverbs when describing Inspector Tweede's actions. Look at those listed below and complete a copy of the table to explain the effect of each.

Evidence	Effect
'mull the facts'	The verb …
'puffing his pipe'	The verb …
'copious notes'	The adjective 'copious' suggests that he writes down as many details as he can in order to solve the case.
'gingerly'	The adverb …
'he deduced'	

3 The poet uses lists in some of the stanzas. For example, the list 'In his tweed suit, tweed cape, tweed deerstalker's cap and ever-present pipe' suggests Inspector Tweede has a lot of accessories traditionally associated with Sherlock Holmes. This creates the impression that he is a great detective. Find other examples of lists in the poem and explain their effect.

4 The poet uses exclamation marks at the end of many of the poem's lines. Find three examples of these and explain why the poet might have used them.

NOW TRY THIS

1 The death of Percival Hoar occurred on a 'dark and stormy night'. Write a paragraph describing a stormy scene at night. Use adjectives, adverbs and figurative language to make the description vivid.

2 Imagine you are Inspector Tweede, writing about your memories after you have retired from the police force. Write a diary entry describing your thoughts and feelings about what happened on the night of the discovery of Percival Hoar's body and how you solved the most high-profile case of your career. You might like to use this opening:

> I can remember that night as if it was yesterday …

FAST FINISHERS

The poet uses 'dastardly' and 'terrible' when describing the 'deed'. Use a thesaurus to make a list of some interesting synonyms for the word 'terrible'. Next, use the thesaurus to make a list of some interesting antonyms for 'terrible'.

3 Imagine that Inspector Tweede has become a minor celebrity after successfully solving the death of Percival Hoar. A television station wishes to interview him about his crime-solving abilities and the cases he has worked on. With a partner, role play an interview with Inspector Tweede.

❓ PRACTICE QUESTION

Read the extract again. Choose **four** statements below which are **true**. [4 marks]

* Copy out the ones that you think are true.
* Choose a maximum of four true statements.

A Inspector Tweede's name is Peter. ☐

B Percival Hoar is a fictional prime minister. ☐

C Inspector Tweede started his career as an office worker. ☐

D His suit is made of tweed. ☐

E Percival Hoar was murdered by his butler. ☐

F Inspector Tweede wears a bowler hat. ☐

G Percival Hoar liked to drink rum. ☐

H Inspector Tweede shouted 'Eureka!' when he had solved the case. ☐

21 Flannan Isle

by Wilfrid Wilson Gibson

LEARNING OBJECTIVES

- To distinguish main ideas and select relevant points from the text.
- To explore how the writer creates mood and atmosphere.
- To analyse the writer's use of language and techniques in a poem.

CONTEXT

'Flannan Isle' is about a true incident that involved three lighthouse keepers who vanished mysteriously from Flannan Isle, a remote island off the west coast of Scotland. No one else lived on the island so there were no witnesses to say what happened to them. The lighthouse keepers had been sent to the island to ensure that the light would never be turned off and the lighthouse would not be left unattended. The following extract from the poem begins with a search party of three men entering the lighthouse on Flannan Isle to investigate what has happened.

The poem is written as a ballad. This means that it tells a story and is written in stanzas with a clear rhyme scheme.

Yet all too soon we reached the door –
The black sun-blistered lighthouse-door
That gaped for us ajar.
As on the threshold for a spell
We paused, we seemed to breathe the smell
Of limewash and of tar,
Familiar as our daily breath,
As though 'twere some strange scent of death:
And so yet wondering side by side
We stood a moment still tongue-tied,
And each with black foreboding eyed
The door ere we should fling it wide
To leave the sunlight for the gloom:
Till, plucking courage up, at last
Hard on each other's heels we passed
Into the living-room.

Yet as we crowded through the door
We only saw a table spread
For dinner, meat and cheese and bread,
But all untouched and no one there;
As though when they sat down to eat,
Ere they could even taste,
Alarm had come and they in haste
Had risen and left the bread and meat,

> The search party arrive at the lighthouse. The adjectives 'black' and 'sun-blistered' create a negative and fearful atmosphere.

> There is a creepy, unnerving feeling that makes the men nervous and unable to speak.

> The men investigating have to pluck up courage to enter the room.

For at the table-head a chair
Lay tumbled on the floor.

We listened, but we only heard
The feeble cheeping of a bird
That starved upon its perch;
And, listening still, without a word
We set about our hopeless search.
We hunted high, we hunted low,
And soon ransacked the empty house;
Then o'er the Island to and fro
We ranged, to listen and to look
In every cranny, cleft or nook
That might have hid a bird or mouse:
But though we searched from shore to shore
We found no sign in any place,
And soon again stood face to face
Before the gaping door,
And stole into the room once more
As frightened children steal.
Ay, though we hunted high and low
And hunted everywhere,
Of the three men's fate we found no trace
Of any kind in any place
But a door ajar, and an untouched meal
And an overtoppled chair.

And as we listened in the gloom
Of that forsaken living-room –
A chill clutch on our breath –
We thought how ill-chance came to all
Who kept the Flannan Light,
And how the rock had been the death
Of many a likely lad –
How six had come to a sudden end
And three had gone stark mad,
And one, whom we'd all known as friend,
Had leapt from the lantern one still night
And fallen dead by the lighthouse wall –
And long we thought
On the three we sought,
And on what might yet befall.

Like curs a glance has brought to heel
We listened, flinching there,
And looked and looked on the untouched meal
And the overtoppled chair.

We seemed to stand for an endless while,
Though still no word was said,
Three men alive on Flannan Isle
Who thought on three men dead.

The investigators search everywhere for the missing men and for possible clues about what might have occurred.

Inside they find an unusual scene that makes them worry about what has happened to the lighthouse men.

The bird had been abandoned and was almost starving to death. The adjective 'feeble' describes the weak condition of the bird.

These are the only clues they can find.

The investigators become scared as they remember that mysterious things have happened to people who have worked at the Flannan Isle lighthouse.

What might the men be worried about here?

At the end, they come to the conclusion that the lighthouse men are dead.

GLOSSARY

Isle: island

Sun-blistered: scorched by the sun

Gaped for us ajar: stood open for us

On the threshold, for a spell: on the entrance for a minute

Limewash: a type of paint

'Twere: it was

Scent: smell

Tongue tied: unable to speak

Foreboding: a feeling that something bad will happen

Ere: before

In haste: in a hurry

Ransacked: rummaged through

O'er: over

Cleft: hole

Ranged: moved around

Stole: crept

Steal: creep

Aye: yes

Ill chance: bad luck

Likely lad: hopeful boy

Sought: looked for

Befall: happened

Curs: dogs

SKILLS FOCUS

✔ Understand how the poet creates mood and atmosphere.

✔ Analyse the writer's use of language.

✔ Produce a piece of descriptive writing.

LOOK CLOSER

1. Read the poem again. Think of a title for each stanza that summarises its events.

2. Write a list of the clues that suggest that something strange has happened at the lighthouse.

3. The poet uses some interesting words and phrases to create mood and atmosphere. Copy and complete the table below and explain what mood is created by these phrases.

Evidence	Explanation
'some strange scent of death'	The adjective 'strange' suggests something unusual has happened and the mood becomes unnerving. The word 'death' makes the mood seem …
'black foreboding'	
'to leave the sunlight for the gloom'	
'as frightened children steal'	
'forsaken living-room'	
'we listened flinching there'	

NOW TRY THIS

1 You are one of the men investigating this mysterious scene and strange disappearance. Write the report that you would give to the police when you return. Remember to include the facts, as you far as you know them. What would your conclusion be as to what has happened to the lighthouse men?

2 Write a description of a mysterious or creepy building. In order to make your description interesting and vivid, use:

- adjectives
- similes
- metaphors
- personification.

FAST FINISHERS

Turn your description into a poem! Think about:

- the number of stanzas
- the length of the lines
- repetition
- whether or not you want the poem to rhyme.

3 You and the other investigators are being interviewed by a news programme about your experiences when investigating the strange case of Flannan Isle. With your partner, plan, prepare and write a script for the interview.

Be prepared to act out the interview in front of the class.

❓ PRACTICE QUESTION

Read the extract again. Choose **four** statements below which are **true**. [4 marks]

- Copy out the ones that you think are true.
- Choose a maximum of four true statements.

A Five men had been sent to investigate the disappearances. ☐

B The lighthouse door is painted blue. ☐

C The lighthouse men had left their meal untouched. ☐

D In the past, three lighthouse men had gone mad. ☐

E A chair had been overturned. ☐

F The pet bird was dead. ☐

G There was no trace of what had happened to the three lighthouse men. ☐

H Flannan Isle is a village. ☐

▲ Some of the items found in the victim's pockets

LEARNING OBJECTIVES

- To distinguish main ideas and select relevant points from the text.
- To recognise explicit and implicit meanings.
- To analyse the writer's use of language and techniques in a poem.

CONTEXT

Simon Armitage is a well-known English poet, born in Yorkshire in 1963. He became the British Poet Laureate in May 2019. Poet Laureate is a respected, honorary position whereby the poet is expected to write poetry for important national occasions.

This poem is about the discovery of a body and is a monologue from the point of view of a police officer. The title 'About His Person' is referring to the items found on the dead person that would be logged and listed by the police. The poem is set out like the clues in a detective story where the reader has to try to work out what has happened.

Why has the man suggested that the dates in his diary from 24 March to 1 April are important? What do you think might have happened?

We know the man has taken his wedding ring off because the skin underneath has not been exposed to the weather.

Five pounds fifty in change, exactly,
a library card on its date of expiry.

A postcard stamped,
unwritten, but franked,

a pocket size diary slashed with a pencil
from March twenty-fourth to the first of April.

A brace of keys for a mortise lock,
an analogue watch, self winding, stopped.

A final demand
in his own hand,

a rolled up note of explanation
planted there like a spray carnation

but beheaded, in his fist.
A shopping list.

A give away photograph stashed in his wallet,
a keepsake banked in the heart of a locket.

no gold or silver,
but crowning one finger

a ring of white unweathered skin.
That was everything.

This is a formal list of the items that were found on the man's body.

The man's watch has stopped. What do you think might have caused this?

The top of the note has been cut off.

GLOSSARY

Expiry: ending

Franked: marked to show postage has been paid

Slashed: cut

Brace: a pair of

Mortise lock: a secure door lock

Analogue watch: a watch with figures and hands which the wearer has to wind up

Final demand: a request for money from a company you owe

Spray carnation: a little flower

Beheaded: with the top cut off

Stashed: hidden

Keepsake: a reminder of someone or something

Unweathered: not exposed to the weather

SKILLS FOCUS

✔ Recognise explicit and implicit meanings.

✔ Understand and analyse the writer's use of language.

✔ Produce a piece of writing with an appropriate format and tone.

LOOK CLOSER

1 Choose one clue from each stanza and suggest what you think each might tell us about the man and his actions. Copy and complete the table below. An example has been completed to help you.

	Clue	Explanation
1	'library card on its date of expiry'	This suggests the police know his name as it would be on the card but he didn't intend to renew the book as it was ending on that day.
2	'A postcard stamped, unwritten'	
3		
4		
5		
6		
7		
8		
9		
10		

2 We never find out what has happened to the man. There are suggestions that he has left his wife because there are words that remind the reader of things coming to an end. Write a list of these words.

3 Write down three examples of words and phrases you find interesting in the poem and explain the effect they have on you. Copy and complete a table like the one below. An example has been completed below.

Example	Explanation
'photograph stashed in his wallet'	This phrase interests me because the verb 'stashed' suggests it means a lot to him and he doesn't want to lose it.

NOW TRY THIS

1 Write the diary entries for this man for Wednesday 24 March to Wednesday 1 April. What do you think happened on those days? What would he be thinking and feeling? You might want to start with the following line:

I can't believe what has happened! Today's events will change my life forever ...

2 Write a front-page newspaper report about the discovery of the man's body and the police appeal for any information. Think about:

☺ the layout and headline

☺ important details like who, where, what, when, why.

THE NEWSPAPER

HEADLINE GOES HERE

FAST FINISHERS

POST CARD

FOR CORRESPONDENCE | FOR ADDRESS

We don't know who the postcard was from or who it might have been sent to. Draw a postcard and write the message you think would have been written on it.

3 What items are currently in your bag or pockets? What do these items suggest about you and your life? Choose three of these items and explain to the class what they are, why you need them and what they show about you.

❓ PRACTICE QUESTION

Read the poem again. How has Armitage used language to make the poem interesting? Write at least three paragraphs in response. Here are some sentence starters to help you with your first paragraph:

⭐ Firstly, Armitage uses ...

⭐ For example, he writes ...

⭐ This makes the poem seem mysterious because ...   [8 marks]

23 The Man Who Finds Out His Son Has Become a Thief

by Raymond Souster

▲ A shoplifter

LEARNING OBJECTIVES

- To distinguish main ideas and select relevant points from the text.
- To consider the structure of a poem.
- To analyse the writer's use of language and techniques in a poem.

CONTEXT

Raymond Souster (1921–2012) was a well-known Canadian poet. During his lifetime, he wrote more than 50 volumes of poetry. This poem is written in five stanzas of different lengths. Some lines are quite short while others are longer, and there is no rhyme, perhaps to show the father's shock at finding out the news about his son.

The son pleads his innocence to his father and the owner.

The father starts to calm down as he realises his anger isn't helping the situation. He listens to the evidence from the shop owner but he finds it difficult to hear.

The father now wants to leave as quickly as possible and to be alone. Why do you think he wants to do this?

Coming into the store at first angry
At the accusation, believing in
The word of the boy who has told him:
I didn't steal anything, honest.

Then becoming calmer, seeing that anger
Will not help in the business, listening painfully
As the other's evidence unfolds, so painfully slow.

Then seeing gradually that evidence
Almost as if tighten slowly around the neck
Of his son, at first vaguely circumstantial, then
    gathering damage
Until there is present the unmistakable odour of guilt
Which seeps now into the mind and lays its poison.

Suddenly feeling sick and alone and afraid,
As if an unseen hand had slapped him in the face
For no reason whatsoever, wanting to get out
Into the street, the night, the darkness, anywhere to hide
The pain that must show in the face to these strangers,
    the fear.

It must be like this.
It could hardly be otherwise.

A father finds out his son has been accused of stealing from a shop. He believes in the innocence of his son and goes to the shop to confront the owner.

Suddenly, the father begins to doubt his son's innocence.

The evidence against the son becomes obvious and the father realises his son has lied to him.

The father is now totally convinced that his son is guilty.

GLOSSARY

Accusation: blame

Vaguely: slightly

Circumstantial: something that hasn't been proven

Odour: smell

Seeps: drips

SKILLS FOCUS

✔ Analyse the writer's use of language and imagery.

✔ Produce a piece of lively creative writing.

✔ Listen and respond appropriately to others.

LOOK CLOSER

1 Write a summary of what happens in the poem in only 60 words. Copy and complete the following table with your summary by writing one word in each box.

At	first							

2 The poem contains several language features. Fill in a copy of the table below, analysing the language that the poet uses.

Evidence	Language feature	Explanation
'evidence / Almost as if tighten slowly around the neck'	personification	
'unmistakable odour of guilt'	metaphor	
'lays its poison'	metaphor	
'As if an unseen hand had slapped him in the face'	simile	

3 Track the father's changing emotions as you read through the poem. Fill in a copy of the table below with your evidence.

Stanza	Father's feelings	Evidence
1	Incensed/furious	'at first / Angry at the accusation'
2		
3		
4		
5		

4 In stanza 4, there is a lot of enjambement. Why does the poet use this technique in this stanza and what does it suggest about the how the father is feeling at this point?

NOW TRY THIS

1 The father is clearly devastated by what his son has done and also the fact that his son has lied to him. Write the father's diary entry about the events of that evening. Make sure that you explain and describe his feelings in detail. You might want to start with the following line:

> I still can't believe what happened tonight. My whole world has been turned upside down!

2 The son finally admits his crime to both his father and the police. Write his confession. You might want to start with the following line:

> I don't know why I decided to do it really. I should have known that I would be letting my family down ...

FAST FINISHERS

What qualities do you think make a good parent/child relationship? Produce a leaflet listing the Ten Golden Rules that would help create a good parent/child relationship.

3 The father has to go home and explain to his wife what has happened. With a partner, prepare and act out the conversation between them. Be ready to perform the scene in front of the class.

4 Imagine that the father has been asked to speak about his son in court. Although the father now knows that his son is guilty, he would still want to talk about his usual good character. What would he say to defend his son?

❓ PRACTICE QUESTION

How does the poet change the mood of the poem to interest the reader? Write a paragraph about each stanza in your answer. Here are some sentence starters to help you:

✪ **Stanza 1**

At the start of the poem, there is a _____ mood.

For example, the poet writes ...

This makes the poem interesting because ...

✪ **Stanza 2**

In the second stanza of the poem, the mood changes and becomes ...

For example, the poet writes ...

This intrigues the reader because ...

✪ **Stanza 3**

In the next part, the mood is ...

For example, the poet ...

I think the mood has changed from the beginning because ...

✪ **Stanza 4**

We know that the father's feelings have changed because ...

The simile _____ suggests the mood has become ...

✪ **Stanza 5**

Finally ...

[8 marks]

▲ The black cat with 'round eyes mad as gold'

CONTEXT

Vernon Scannell (1922–2007) was a British poet who was once a professional boxer. He began by writing poems about sport but then widened the topics he covered and had 53 poems published.

'A Case of Murder' is not divided into stanzas and has an irregular rhyme scheme.

They should not have left him alone,
Alone that is except for the cat.
He was only nine, not old enough
To be left alone in a **basement** flat,
Alone, that is, except for the cat. ◄ · · · · · · A nine-year-old boy is left alone with a pet cat that he hates.
A dog would have been a different thing,
A big gruff dog with **slashing** jaws,
But a cat with round eyes mad as gold,
Plump as a cushion with tucked-in paws –
Better have left him with a fair-sized rat! ◄ · · · · He hates the cat so much that he would rather have been left with a fierce dog or a rat.
But what they did was leave him with a cat.
He hated that cat; he watched it sit,
A buzzing machine of soft black stuff,
He sat and watched and he hated it,
Snug in its fur, hot blood in a **muff**,
And its mad gold stare and the way it sat
Crooning dark warmth: he **loathed** all that.
So he took Daddy's stick and he hit the cat. ◄ · · · The boy starts to lose his self-control and lashes out at the cat with a stick.
Then quick as a sudden crack in glass
What impression of the cat do we have from the verb 'hissed' as he tries to escape from the boy's attack? · · · ► It **hissed**, black flash, to a hiding place
In the dust and dark beneath the couch,
And he followed the grin on his new-made face,

A wide-eyed, frightened snarl of a grin,
And he took the stick and he thrust it in,
Hard and quick in the furry dark,
The black fur squealed and he felt his skin
Prickle with sparks of dry delight.
Then the cat again came into sight,
Shot for the door that wasn't quite shut,
But the boy, quick too, slammed fast the door:
The cat, half-through, was cracked like a nut
And the soft black thud was dumped on the floor.
Then the boy was suddenly terrified
And he bit his knuckles and cried and cried;
But he had to do something with the dead thing there.
His eyes squeezed beads of salty prayer
But the wound of fear gaped wide and raw;
He dared not touch the thing with his hands
So he fetched a spade and shovelled it
And dumped the load of heavy fur
In the spidery cupboard under the stair
Where it's been for years, and though it died
It's grown in that cupboard and its hot low purr
Grows slowly louder year by year:
There'll not be a corner for the boy to hide
When the cupboard swells and all sides split
And the huge black cat pads out of it.

The boy starts to feel excited by the power and control that he has over his enemy, the cat, so his skin starts to tingle with the thrill.

The boy suddenly realises what he has done and immediately regrets his actions. His actions here and the repetition of 'cried and cried' emphasise how terrified he now feels. All his power and excitement have left him.

As the cat tries to escape, the boy shuts the door on him and kills him.

The boy hides the cat's body so he can try to forget what he has done.

The message of the poem is at the end and it shows that you can't hide from your guilty conscience or escape your actions.

GLOSSARY

Basement: lower ground floor
Slashing: fierce
Muff: fur tube to keep hands warm
Crooning: humming/singing softly
Loathed: hated

SKILLS FOCUS

✔ Understand how the poet creates mood and atmosphere.
✔ Analyse the writer's use of language.
✔ Produce a piece of lively creative writing.

LOOK CLOSER

1 Copy and complete the table below to explain what impression these similes and metaphors give of the cat.

Evidence	Language feature	Effect
'round eyes mad as gold'	simile	This simile makes the cat seem …
'plump as a cushion'		
'a buzzing machine'	metaphor	
'cracked like a nut'		

2 Scannell creates a changing mood and atmosphere in the poem. Copy and complete the table below to explain what mood is created by these quotes.

Evidence	Effect
'watched it sit'	The verb 'watched' creates a tense mood as the boy is staring at the cat.
'he sat and watched and hated it'	
'quick as a sudden crack in glass'	
'he took the stick and thrust it in'	

3 At the end of the poem, how does the poet suggest that the boy is now scared and regrets what he has done? Copy and complete the table to organise your ideas and then write your evidence in a paragraph.

Evidence	Effect
'then the boy was suddenly terrified'	The adverb 'suddenly' suggests that the boy is really shocked by what he has done. The adjective 'terrified' makes us think that …
'he bit his knuckles'	
'he cried and cried'	
'his eyes squeezed beads of salty prayer'	
'the wound of fear gaped wide and raw'	

NOW TRY THIS

1. Write an account of a time when you did something you were ashamed of. Remember to think about:
   - what happened
   - how you felt after the incident
   - whether you were caught or if you owned up about what you had done.

2. Write the boy's diary entry about the incident with the cat and how he felt afterwards.

   You might want to start with the following line:

   I don't know why I did it. I never really meant to hurt the cat and now I feel …

FAST FINISHERS

The poet uses many similes and metaphors to describe the cat. Write a description of an animal using similes and metaphors.

3. The boy finally decides to confess to his parents what has happened. With a partner, prepare and act out the conversation that takes place.

4. The incident has been reported to the police. Prepare the speech that the boy would make to defend himself and his actions. Read it out to the class.

❓ PRACTICE QUESTION

What impression do we have of the boy in the poem? Write four paragraphs. Here are some sentence starters to help you:

- **Paragraph 1**

  At the start of the poem, the boy is described as …

  For example, the poet writes …

  This makes the boy seem … because …

- **Paragraph 2**

  In the next section, the boy starts to feel …

  For example, the poet writes …

  This creates the impression that …

- **Paragraph 3**

  In the next part, the boy becomes …

  For example, the poet …

  I think the boy's behaviour has changed from the beginning because …

- **Paragraph 4**

  Finally, …   [8 marks]

Key terms

Active verb	When the person or thing does something, rather than has an action done to them.
Adjective	A word that describes a noun, e.g. the reckless man.
Adverb	A word that describes a verb, e.g. he ran hastily.
Alliteration	When two or more words begin with the same letter or sound, e.g. 'Jolly giant giraffes jest joyfully in June'.
Anecdote	A story from the writer's own personal experience.
Bildungsroman	A story told from a young character's point of view which charts their development as they change and grow.
Compare	To find similar qualities between ideas.
Context	Background information about the writer or the time the text is set.
Contrast	To have very different qualities to something else.
Dialogue	A conversation between two or more people.
Dramatic irony	When the significance of the character's words or actions is clear to the audience but unknown to the character.
Ellipsis	A set of dots that usually indicates a pause or that words have been intentionally missed out. (Note: the plural is ellipses.)
Emotive language	Language that appeals to a reader's emotions.
End rhyme	Rhyme between a poem's line endings.
Enjambement	In poetry, where a sentence continues from one line to the next line without a pause.
Explicit information	Information that is stated clearly.
Figurative language	Language such as similes, metaphors or personification.
Foreshadowing	When later events in a story are hinted at before they happen.
Imagery	The use of language to create word pictures by comparing one thing with another; see also metaphor, personification, simile.
Imperative	A command or request.
Implicit information	Information that is implied, rather than stated clearly.
Internal rhyme	Rhyme that occurs within a single line of a poem.
Juxtaposition	Putting two contrasting ideas next to each other.
Metaphor	When a word or phrase is used to describe something else, e.g. 'She was on fire', to suggest that she is very good at what she is doing.
Mood	The atmosphere of a piece of writing, e.g. scary, peaceful, exciting, dull, sad.
Narrative approach	First person (I walked), second person (You walked) or third person (He/She/They walked).
Noun	An object, e.g. chair, name, e.g. Sarah, or emotion, e.g. love.
Onomatopoeia	When a word sounds like the sound it describes, e.g. Bang!
Paraphrase	Expressing the meaning of something by using different words.
Pathetic fallacy	Where the weather (or other inanimate object) reflects what is happening in a story.
Personification	Describing something that isn't human by using human qualities, e.g. 'The tree danced in the wind'.
Pronoun	A word used in place of a noun or someone's name, e.g. I, you, she, they, my, our, themselves.
Protagonist	One of the major characters in a story.
Quotation	Taking a group of words from a text or speech.
Repetition	Repeating a word or phrase to make it memorable.
Rhetorical question	A question in writing or speech that is used to involve the reader but does not require an answer.
Sibilance	The repetition of 's' sounds for effect, e.g. 'The sly and sinister snake'.
Simile	When something is compared to something else using the words 'like' or 'as', e.g. 'As snug as a bug', 'Cold like ice'.
Tone	The attitude of a writer towards the subject or his audience, e.g. funny, sad, formal, informal, sarcastic.
Verb	An action word, e.g. running, walked, dances.